PRAISE FOR SOUL JOURNEYS

"Since the emergence in 2000 of the first book in a trilogy that became a publishing phenomenon by Philip Pullman, the *His Dark Materials* series, the idea of a daemon, a manifestation of a person's soul in the form of an animal, has gripped the imagination of millions of readers, young and old.

"Now authors Dan Prechtel, John Mabry, and Katrina Leathers have given us the gift of an exploration of the intersection of shamanic worlds, where spirit guides, often in animal forms, are prominent, and the world of Christian theology and practice. In their new book, *Soul Journeys: Christian Spirituality and Shamanism as Pathways to Wholeness and Understanding*, Prechtel, Mabry and Leathers bring these two venerable and vital spiritual paths together to create a synergy that will help the reader chart a new way to a whole and sustainable life.

"It is possible that readers who are committed to either path —shamanism or Christianity—may be hesitant about the encounter opened by this book. I want to assure the readers that the authors tread with great respect for both traditions. There is risk in reading this book, but it is the golden risk of opening our lives to new possibilities. I encourage you to read *Soul Journeys*."

—Bishop Marc Andrus, Episcopal Diocese of California

"Soul Journeys invites us into the dynamic, expansive horizons of spiritual possibilities. Through personal, historical, scriptural, and literary threads, the authors creatively weave together Christian spirituality and core shamanism, with a call to commune with ourselves and the cosmos with greater intimacy."

—Cynthia Li, MD, integrative doctor and author of *Brave New Medicine*

"Both fascinating and informative, I believe this book will inspire people of the Christian and various faith traditions who are longing for their own direct spiritual experiences. It challenges us to go beyond the reductionist, intellectual and doctrinal limitations of Christianity. I have found it to offer new and highly personal ways to live out my faith. I hope that many will find it to be food for their spiritual growth."

—The Reverend Dr. Bradley Hauff, Indigenous Ministries Missioner for The Episcopal Church

"What spiritualities will emerge to slake our thirst for authentic spiritual practice as institutional, hierarchical Christianity continues its fast fade in the West? Jung recommended alchemy and gnosis. Zen and other Buddhist forms have helped many. Others have advocated for various liberation spiritualities, a Wisdom Jesus, the cosmic Christ, and more. In this humble, practical, thoughtful book, Prechtel, Mabry, and Leathers make a compelling case for shamanism being another arrow that belongs in our emerging, post-Christian spiritual quiver. I found their work—especially their experienced, collaborative voices—consistently engaged me."

—The Rev. Stephen Martz, DMin, Episcopal priest, past president of the Chicago Society of Jungian Analysts.

"*Soul Journeys* provides a profound conversation between shamanic practice and experiences of Christian prayer. We are guided by seasoned practitioners, with deep theological understanding. Ancient practices of Christian life are animated in fresh ways through this conversation. The energies of the earth, often neglected in Christian practice, are given voice through Shamanic understanding. We are encouraged to embrace the interior life through the prayer of the imagination of St. Ignatius of Loyola and claim again the interface between ordinary human experience and the Divine eternal realm. We are invited to receive Holy Communion as the "medicine of immortality," participate in Liturgics of Healing Prayer, and seek out Shamanic healers in our personal journey toward wholeness."

—Rev. Dwight H. Judy, PhD, Professor Emeritus of Spiritual Formation, Garrett-Evangelical Theological Seminary, Evanston, IL. Author of *Embracing God: Praying with Teresa of Avila*.

SOUL JOURNEYS

CHRISTIAN SPIRITUALITY AND SHAMANISM AS PATHWAYS FOR WHOLENESS AND UNDERSTANDING

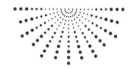

DANIEL L. PRECHTEL   JOHN R. MABRY

KATRINA LEATHERS

APOCRYPHILE
PRESS

Apocryphile Press
1700 Shattuck Ave #81
Berkeley, CA 94709
www.apocryphilepress.com

Copyright © 2020 by Daniel Prechtel, John R. Mabry & Katrina Leathers
Printed in the United States of America
ISBN 978-1-949643-47-3 | paperback
ISBN 978-1-949643-48-0 | epub

Please join our mailing list at
www.apocryphilepress.com/free
We'll keep you up-to-date on all our new releases,
and we'll also send you a FREE BOOK. Visit us today!

CONTENTS

ACKNOWLEDGMENTS

The big things are not done by ourselves alone. We draw on those who go before us and those who support us in our work. It was a big help, and an enjoyable experience, for the three of us to work together on this project, but there were many more who aided in creating this book. Our own spiritual directors, colleagues, teachers, and others who support us deserve our grateful thanks. There are also those helping spirits, that "great cloud of witnesses," that provide us with the grace and spiritual power to do our work. We wish to give special thanks to the following persons (listed in no particular order) who took time to read and provide thoughtful questions and feedback: Patricia Terry, Eric Prechtel, Hans Prechtel, Diane Martineau, Bradley Hauff, Bude VanDyke, Aida Merriweather, Kathie McCutcheon, Martha O'Hehir, Martha Stortz, Mary Linda McKinney, Megan Humlie, and Laura Rolen. Also, deep gratitude to the dear people who consented to have their shamanic healing stories shared.

INTRODUCTION

DANIEL L. PRECHTEL

At a spiritual direction peer supervision meeting several years ago I expressed my frustration that many people who are mainline Christians either seem ignorant of the powerful spiritual realities and resources of their tradition or afraid to claim them for fear of judgment by others. I questioned how well our churches and clergy educated the people in their charge and wished aloud that we would write a book about this. My spiritual direction colleagues, all clergy from mainline denominations, nodded their heads. Two spoke up that they would be interested in helping to write such a book. One of them, John Mabry, continued with me in the writing project. The other colleague sadly suffered the death of her beloved spouse and needed to withdraw.

John was my first professional contact as a spiritual direction colleague in the Bay Area after I moved from Evanston, Illinois in 2009. He invited me to join the peer supervision group that he attended. Later John invited me to teach and supervise some trainees in the Chaplaincy Institute's interfaith spiritual direction program in Berkeley. John brings a wealth of knowledge in comparative religions as well as many years of Christian pastoral and interfaith spiritual direction experience to our conversation.

In the meantime I was laboring to integrate the powerful experiences I had undergone in training in Core Shamanism[1] with my Christian religious beliefs and spiritual experiences. I had met Katrina Leathers in my work for the Chaplaincy Institute and learned of her extensive training through the Foundation for Shamanic Studies where I was studying. We began meeting once a month for mutual support, reflection, and journeying as shamanic practitioners. Katrina, who is not a Christian, listened patiently as I brought in parallels from Christian spiritual practices or expressed my desire to explore the commonalities between Core Shamanism and my own faith tradition. I invited Katrina to join the writing project due to her long experience with Core Shamanism and her interfaith ministry and spiritual direction practice. Katrina brings profound heart and depth, including shamanism as her primary spirituality, to the conversation.

In the beginning of the project I wondered about comparing Christian and Core Shamanism orientations and practices alongside Jungian and post-Jungian depth psychology. To that end I had several conversations with an Episcopal priest who was also a clinical psychologist with a Jungian orientation. The question was also raised about adding another religious tradition's perspective to our exploration. Both these perspectives would bring additional richness to our study, but also bring much more complexity. I ended up deciding to keep the focus restricted to Christian spirituality and shamanism. Perhaps this project will serve as a model and encourage dialogue between Core Shamanism and other religious traditions and psychological perspectives.

There have been other writers that brought me creative conversations between Christian spirituality and other ways of perceiving and engaging reality. Episcopal priests Morton

Kelsey and John Sanford brought Jungian analytical psychology into dialogue with Christian prayer and meditation and biblical interpretation. Kelsey also wrote in the early 1980s about what a modern Christian shaman would be like. Jesuit priest William Johnston engaged Zen Buddhist methods and Christian mysticism. William Stolzman reported on a six-year dialogue of Roman Catholic pastors and medicine men on the Rosebud Reservation. Others also have written on the interaction between spiritual traditions and their practices.

I am particularly grateful to have read *The Way of All the Earth: Experiments in Truth and Religion* by the late John S. Dunne, professor of theology at Notre Dame University, in my first year of seminary. Dunne wrote of his experiments in "passing over" into the lives, cultures, and truths of great religious figures such as Jesus Christ, Mohandas Gandhi, Gautama Buddha, and Mohammad and returning again with an enriched understanding of Christian faith. Dunne set the example for me to take the risk of respectfully journeying into other perspectives and lived traditions to grow and learn and bring back the truths I am able to share.

By bringing Core Shamanism and Christian spirituality into dialogue it is our hope that readers will be more aware of ways we can knowingly participate in the vast, wonderful, and mysterious worlds of spiritual reality that affect our ordinary life. Some readers will not be familiar with Christianity or have only experienced the fundamentalist or militant expressions of this religion. John and I wish to provide a view of the Christian faith that celebrates its compassionate, mystical, unitive, and healing dimensions, in which we do our best to work in partnership with the Holy Spirit toward the fulfillment of Jesus's prayer petition, "...Thy kingdom come, thy will be done on earth as it is in heaven."

Our view of Christian spirituality does not deny or gloss over the sins and shortcomings of the Church, past and present.

There are things that call for repentance and amendment. Yet we want readers to be aware of the great spiritual treasures and resources God provides in following the way of love that Jesus shows and participating in the creative work of the Spirit. We seek a more expansive Christian spirituality than is usually envisioned, taught, or practiced.

Shamanism is a subject of great interest in the general spiritual climate of our time. This subject elicits a whole spectrum of responses, sometimes accompanied by powerful feelings ranging from fear and deep suspicion to fascination and excitement. There are many varieties of shamanic teaching and practice. Many are deeply embedded in the ethos and experience of a particular indigenous people. These shamanic cultures deserve respect and integrity. Replication of selected beliefs and practices of a particular shamanic culture—without the consent of their own authorities—by shamanic teachers and practitioners of the culturally-dominant white European-American population, no matter how well-intentioned, can cross the line and become spiritual and cultural misappropriation.

When we discuss shamanism there are several additional things to bear in mind. While both Katrina and I have received advanced training in Core Shamanism through the Foundation for Shamanic Studies, we speak from our own personal experience and not as authorized representatives of that organization. We are very grateful for their teaching programs and recommend the Foundation as an excellent way to experientially learn about the fascinating worlds of shamanism and how to become a shamanic practitioner. However, our own methods and understanding may differ somewhat from the methods we were originally taught (or read from Michael Harner's books) for various reasons.

Teaching and experiential methods within the Foundation for Shamanic Studies continue to change and evolve as more is learned and tested out with students. The Foundation aims to bring Core Shamanism to a primarily Western culture while honoring and supporting indigenous shamanic cultural experience. Their founder, the late cultural anthropologist Michael Harner, developed programs to train students in "core shamanism," teaching shamanic methods and orientations that are universally, near universally, or commonly practiced by shamanic cultures. In my experience the Foundation is sensitive to, and guards against, cultural or spiritual misappropriation by restricting their practice methods to those that are shared cross-culturally. I see Core Shamanism as bringing those of us with a Western cultural heritage the basic shamanic tools and orientation that were largely lost over many centuries of persecution in Western Europe and the British Isles by the dominant political and religious powers of the times.

As shamanic practitioners we continue to learn directly from our own spirit helpers and teachers. These spirits intimately know what is best suited to our particular needs, situations, and capacities. A training program is designed to give us the basics, but our own particular methods and understandings develop over time from our interactions with our spirit helpers and teachers. From the shamanic perspective the primary teachers are not other shamanic practitioners; rather, they are our spirit allies.

Katrina and I have been informed by other writers and teachers outside the Foundation. Some of these have been former Foundation teachers who have gone on to develop their own programs and have written about their experiences. My understanding and application of healing methods, especially related to what the Christian spiritual tradition calls exorcism and deliverance ministry, has been influenced by research into "spirit releasement therapy" as well as "compassionate depossession" shamanic practices taught by Betsy Bergstrom.

Shamanic journey and Christian visualization practices are very powerful spiritual tools and should be treated with care and respect. Michael Harner used to say that the shaman needs to be the master of both worlds: the worlds of ordinary and nonordinary reality. We should be well-grounded in our ability to differentiate which reality we are in and have the requisite knowledge and capacity to act appropriately in each one. Those who lack that ability, whether because of inexperience, mental and emotional distress, trauma, or some other vulnerability, should refrain from making such forays into non-ordinary reality unless they are guided by someone who is experienced and knowledgeable. It is best for anyone to have a spiritual guide or other competent person to provide backup support when venturing into spiritual realities beyond ordinary consciousness.

We do not want to make the assumption that all our readers will be familiar with Christianity and with shamanism. There will be some who are, and many who might be somewhat familiar with one or the other spiritual tradition presented. But again, our purpose is to look at both traditions through the lens of lived experience and dialogue.

I will provide an introduction to Core Shamanism in Chapter 1: *Journeys to the Worlds of Spirits*. Here I give basic information on the subject of shamanism and describe the worlds and their beings according to my understanding of Core Shamanism. This will be different than a presentation on shamanism coming from an indigenous cultural perspective, which I cannot represent. I also introduce some comparisons with Christianity and describe some of the historical tensions with this religion.

In Chapter 2: *The Visionary and Shamanistic in Christian Tradition*, John Mabry gives scriptural, historical, literary, and liturgical visionary elements with similarities to shamanism. John also addresses the importance of the disciplined use of imagination as a vehicle for visionary experience and access to spirit realities.

After this foundation, each of us in Chapters 3-5 offers personal stories that describe and reflect upon our spiritual experiences. Some stories are about our personal lives; others reflect our professional experiences. An overall theme in these chapters is how we have received spiritual guidance and wisdom and/or spiritual healing for ourselves or in our ministry with others.

As we were preparing this book Katrina, John, and I invited feedback and questions from readers of draft sections of our manuscript. Happily, we received many questions—over 100 of them! Some questions were best addressed by amplifying or clarifying what we had already written. That's part of the normal process of book editing. But other readers' questions brought up new thoughts and fresh considerations or had enough meat to them that we all wanted to get in on the conversation. Some questions were variations clustered around a general subject area and we fashioned one question to focus conversation around the subject the readers were curious about. So we decided to create Chapter 6: *Going Deeper—A Conversation between Contributors and Readers* for a conversation between readers and ourselves. We hope you enjoy the conversation and feel like your own thoughts and feelings have been reflected and respected.

Our concluding chapter cannot possibly tie everything into a nice, concise package. Better than that—we invite you to join us in wondering, exploring, and expanding your own vision, and participating in something sacred and far greater than any of us can fully comprehend.

We provide a Glossary for help in understanding specialized language. We also provide articles and visualization guides in the Appendices for deepening your own spiritual practice.

SHAMANIC JOURNEYS TO THE WORLDS OF SPIRITS

DANIEL L. PRECHTEL

WHO IS A SHAMAN?

"*S*haman" is a word that is relatively new to our Western vocabulary, even though it refers to a form of spiritual practitioner that reaches back 30,000-70,000 years. The word shaman is derived from the Siberian Tungusic word *saman*, which means "the one who sees in the dark" or "the one who knows." There have been many other names associated with the shamanic practitioner, including, but not limited to, medicine man or medicine woman, magician, witch doctor, witch, sorcerer, wizard, or seer. Some names arise from the particular indigenous culture that relies on and supports the work of their shamans. Some terms for shaman may also be strongly colored by negative stereotypes arising from contesting religious, societal, or political biases. These other names and the practices surrounding them may share some characteristics with the shamanic practitioner, but not necessarily all characteristics. A medium, for example, enters a trance and can communicate with spirits. Or a prophet can receive divine revelations through dreams or prayer visions. A priest leads people into the presence of the Holy through their participation in powerful rituals. These social or religious roles share some, but not all, elements in common with a shamanic practitioner.

It is likely that our present great religions have their origins in the shamanic experiences of their founders and early leaders. Over time the tendency to accumulate teachings and reflections on the meaning of the stories and their application to later community situations can result in a body of beliefs and institutional structures. However, the shaman is primarily motivated by having direct personal experiences of journeying to spiritual realms rather than by indirectly formulating beliefs about them. That is to say that shamanism is primarily an experiential spirituality rather than a religious system of beliefs. One can hold to a religious faith tradition and still engage in shamanic practices. But shamanism is oriented to gaining experiential knowledge and building working relationships with spirit allies.

What characterizes a shaman (or shamanic practitioner) is the ability to move at will into a shamanic state of consciousness (SSC) and journey into a nonordinary reality—what John Mabry calls "the Otherworld"—inhabited by spirits that assist and empower the practitioner for the purposes of healing or bringing knowledge and guidance to the practitioner or the person or community the practitioner is helping. The shamanic practitioner primarily works in alliance with one or more helping spirits while in a shamanic state of consciousness and is guided and empowered by that spirit.

A shaman is one who is recognized as such by the fruit of their work with others. Does healing occur for those who request the help? Do the divination journeys bring new and helpful information or revelations to those who come to the practitioner seeking guidance? Most practitioners are hesitant to call themselves "shamans" due to the critical social aspects of their work, which requires confirmation of their effectiveness by the community. Given the community's determination of who is a shaman, I prefer to consider myself a "shamanic practitioner."

SHAMANIC STATE OF CONSCIOUSNESS

The shamanic state of consciousness is a trance often induced by a "sonic driver," a term coined by Michael Harner. Although Harner's initial experiences with shamanism in the 1960s were induced by powerful hallucinogenic drugs (plant medicine) he discovered in later cross-cultural studies and contacts that in the vast majority of shamanic cultures, the shamanic state of consciousness is induced by a monotonous rhythm of a drum, rattle, bones, sticks or other percussive sounds at about 3.5-7 beats per second. He found that repetitive drumming within a range of 205-220 beats per minute (3.4-3.6 beats/sec) was particularly effective for him. Some nonpercussive sounds, chants, dancing, or meditative silence can also induce the trance state.[1]

What makes the trance a "shamanic" state of consciousness is the practitioner's focused intention and skillful use of the trance to make a shamanic journey to nonordinary reality with its various worlds. The shamanic practitioner explores those worlds, interacts with the various spirits inhabiting those worlds, or brings a helping spirit into this world as a partner in healing, divination, or for some other reason.

When in the shamanic state of consciousness, a shamanic practitioner "sees" and acts in nonordinary reality. The "seeing" may take various forms and may have varying degrees of clarity, depending on the level of the trance state and the intensity of concentration and focused intention. Sometimes a practitioner may not see with visual clarity, but other senses such as touch, smell, or hearing might be strong. The shamanic state of consciousness is a dreamlike trance state and may have the variations in seeing that we are aware of in our dream states, although the shamanic state of consciousness is most similar to a lucid dreaming state (which can be turned into shamanic dreaming). For those who are not familiar with lucid dreaming, it is that state of consciousness wherein the dreamer is aware of being in a dream and is capable of interacting consciously with the dream scene and its "images" and can make decisions on how to continue to act or shift the dream. However, in lucid dreaming the "images" (or "beings") act independently from the dreamer and should be engaged as such. This is also the case with shamanic practitioner interactions with spirits. Spirits are autonomous beings that have their own existence independent from us.

It is possible for the shamanic practitioner to merge with a helping spirit in a voluntary and temporary form of spirit possession. The merge allows the spirit (usually a power animal) to bring its power and other abilities directly to bear on a situation. While in that merged state a shamanic practitioner is capable of making decisions about what actions are warranted and can choose to stop anything that he or she determines is not the right course of action. The compassionate helping spirit is living outside space and time as we know it and sees the situation and needs from its own perspective. The shamanic practitioner sees the situation as a human being operating on behalf of a client within the suitable limits of the particular culture and time. It is the practitioner's responsibility to make sure any help given in partnership with a helping spirit is appropriate to the client's context.

WORLDS OF THE SHAMAN

Shamanism recognizes that there is an ordinary consensual reality which is socially agreed upon. This ordinary reality is in the "middle" world that we all share. There is another dimension of reality, a "nonordinary" reality, which can be perceived in a shamanic state of consciousness. Nonordinary reality is often experienced by shamanic journeyers as consisting of an Upper and Lower World, with both worlds composed of multiple levels. These are inhabited by powerful, wise, and compassionate spirits who desire to assist us in the Middle World. These spirits are highly evolved beings that are not self-centered nor do they have agendas that serve their own self-interests.

There is also the nonordinary Middle World reality which, although normally unseen, can powerfully affect us in our everyday lives. Unlike the spirits of the Upper and Lower World, these spirits do have their own agendas. Nature spirits might interact with shamanic practitioners in ways that are mutually beneficial. In traditional societies the shaman learned the location of animals that can be hunted from such spirits, and the shaman could gain knowledge of how particular plants can be used for medicine and food. But Middle World spirits are not always friendly and are sometimes dangerously intrusive. Some lower level forms of spirit entities act parasitically on humans and cause various maladies. Higher forms of spirit entities in the nonordinary reality of the Middle World may afflict humans, drawing on the host's vitality and affecting their physical, emotional, spiritual, or mental health. However, Christians and others from religious traditions are in error in their tendency to label all such spirits as demonic. Much more discernment is required to accurately differentiate the kind of spirit and its motivation.

Spirits of deceased humans may also linger in the Middle World either intentionally or because of some disorienting situation such as a traumatic death. Some of these may influence or attach to living humans. There are also spirits in the Middle World that are indifferent or neutral toward humans unless they inadvertently wander into proximity to a human or feel that humans are encroaching on their interests.

The Middle World can be a dangerous place under the sway of powerful spirits with their own personal motivations. And humans who use power abusively may be under the influence of such spirits. But the Middle World is also a beautiful and fascinating place to live. A deepened reverence for this living planet and its many species of life is a natural product of exploring its physical and spiritual vastness. One can appreciate the Genesis creation story where God looks upon what God has made and calls it "good." In so many ways it is good.

The Upper and Lower Worlds, in contrast to the Middle World, are entirely places of benevolence. Many see these realms as in complete alignment with divine purposes, although not everyone assumes there is a divine supreme being caring and working for the destiny of all of these worlds. It is generally recognized that the Upper and Lower Worlds are composed of many levels and the shamanic practitioner can explore at least some of those levels (as well as the vastness of the Middle World).

There are also "Interworld" zones located at the extremes of the Middle World, on the borders of the Upper and Lower Worlds. These are zones where living human spirits sometimes go while in coma or near death or in deep despair or some other extreme state. So the Interworld zones are like holding places for human spirits that are near death, or in an extreme state, or for some of those who have died but not yet made the transition to their next life. I have visited these zones on occasion. The Interworld is a very dark and shadowy place and it is dreary. When I have explored those zones I see many people there that seem depressed and isolated. If I go to visit a particular person I am taken directly to that person by one of my helping spirits, and in those situations I am less likely to see others nearby.

In my first journey to the Interworld (I had no name for the location at that time) I had the intention to visit a person near death who was a member of the parish I attended. His family had given me permission to pray and meditate on his behalf in any way I felt appropriate. I had brought the parishioner's situation to my spirit teacher and he suggested I visit him to assure him of God's care and passage to the next life. I asked my spirit friend Bear to accompany us and lead us to where the dying man's spirit was. It was very dark and misty but I could make out a man ahead of me so I walked in that direction. I came up to him and saw his face very clearly. He seemed happy and I introduced myself as one of the priests of his church. He suffered from dementia so I didn't know if he knew who I was. I told him that his family was okay and were being cared for. I assured him that it was okay for him to go to God when it was the right time. He would know when it was time when he felt the strong pull of God's love—that would be God calling him. I encouraged him to trust God and follow that pull or light. He seemed to understand what I said to him and was at peace with his temporary situation.

In a typical Christian understanding of the Upper World, we might think of angels (including guardian angels), archangels, saints, Jesus, Mary, and Sophia (Wisdom) populating a heavenly realm permeated by the Spirit's presence and power. Sometimes Christians have visionary experiences that put them in touch with these beings. These visions might be spontaneously occurring or arise from deep prayer, meditation states, fasts, or vigils. Our personal ancestors reside in this "heavenly" Otherworld realm and may sometimes visit us in dreams or through imaginal encounters. Christian theology describes the unity of the living and the dead in the love of God through Jesus Christ as the "communion of saints." In Christian mystical experience these heavenly spirit beings—such as Mary or Jesus or an angel —sometimes bring healing or revelations. From a shamanic perspective the Upper World also includes various wise human teachers (tutelary spirits) and other beneficent beings regarded by some as gods and goddesses.

Shamanism, oriented to an animistic understanding of nature and respectful of its powers, has also long known that there is a Lower World inhabited by equally compassionate, wise, powerful beings. These spirit beings usually appear as power animals and are wonderful helpers for humans who live in the Middle World. But like the spirits of the Upper World, they normally require partnership with humans to bring them to the Middle World where they can fully use their power for healing or other helpful purposes. People whose perceptions are formed by indigenous, nature-centered cultures may see their deceased relatives (ancestral spirits) dwelling in the Lower World in a way that Christians would consider "heavenly." For Christians, it might help to think of both the Upper and Lower World as heavenly realms.

In my understanding of Core Shamanism there is not a place that has been located that directly corresponds to the Christian concept of Hell. And within Christianity there are widely divergent opinions about a belief in Hell and what may be its purpose. However, some of the regions of the Interworld zones may have some correspondence to the notion of Hell or Purgatory.

SEEING IN NONORDINARY REALITY

Why does a shamanic practitioner see spirits in a particular form? My own view is that spirits appear to us in ways that our minds can accept and grasp as meaningful. The particular appearance may well be a gloss on a reality that goes beyond our ability to fully comprehend. The form of the appearance may be symbolic, using metaphors shaped by our cultural lens to help the practitioner interpret what is "real." The appearance and its underlying reality might be illustrated by the scripture stories of Jesus' ascension into the heavens on a cloud, or Elijah's riding to heaven on a fiery chariot. Our minds need to see what is occurring in a way that allows us to make meaning. Jesus and Elijah may well have shifted to a new dimension of reality, an "Upper World" or "heavenly realm," and the ancient mind needed to see a cloud or chariot to convey that reality. What we "see" in nonordinary reality and what messages we receive are uniquely, and often metaphorically, adapted to the shamanic practitioner's (or their client's) particular needs and sense of meaning.

SHAMANIC ALLIANCES WITH HELPING SPIRITS

One of the initial tasks of shamanic practitioners is to learn how to make journeys to the Upper or Lower World and build alliances with compassionate spirits in those worlds. In my own experience I have had a number of dreams of lions and bears that gave me a sense that these spirits were reaching out to me. In early shamanic journeys I encountered these animals and befriended them as helping spirits. In truth, Lion and Bear had reached out to me long before I approached them. These power animals have their own personalities and their own particular special gifts. Other helping spirits have come to me through the spirit retrieval work done on my behalf by other shamanic practitioners.

Sometimes a power animal will help me get to a place that I need to go in nonordinary reality. I merge with some spirits in order to do some forms of healing. I seek their counsel in divination (discernment) matters. They protect me when I am in the presence of a Middle World spirit that might harm me.

Other helping spirits that shamanic practitioners may work with are Upper World beings. Angels, beings traditionally understood as gods or goddesses, human ascended masters, and ancestral spirits are part of the Upper World population that a practitioner may encounter. Some of these beings may choose to develop a relationship with the practitioner, and such spirits can provide powerful help for healing or divinatory purposes. Some Upper World spirits may become a shamanic practitioner's teachers.

It is important to realize that these Upper and Lower World helping spirits (whether animal or angelic or ancestral or in some other form) are not self-centered and agenda-filled beings. Rather, they are deeply compassionate and highly evolved beings that, from my perspective and based on my journeying experience, are completely aligned and in harmony with God's divine purposes. They are beings that understand things from a far broader frame of reference than we humans are able to know from our limited Middle World experience. They are not restricted, as we are, to a fixed sense of time and space. They want to help us in our Middle World struggles and aid us in our needs for healing, practical knowledge, wisdom, and wholeness.

ETHICAL CONSIDERATIONS

However, the relationship that is forged is a partnership. In matters related to the Middle World it is the shamanic practitioner that has the final say on what is to be done. Because the helping spirit is visiting from a very different place beyond our normal cultural rules and normal ways of interacting it is the human practitioner that makes the judgments about what is going to actually be helpful for a client. That means that the shamanic practitioner needs to be very careful about how the power offered by the spirit is used. One of the basic tenets is that nothing should be done by a shamanic practitioner to another person without the free and informed consent of that person. In situations involving children or adults incapable of giving consent it must be given by a person authorized to represent their best interests. Even if the "client" is dead and no one can speak on their behalf, as we will discuss in psychopomp work, it still requires the consent of that human spirit.

To act upon another person without their consent risks the dangers of practicing sorcery and abuse of power. Those who use their power by manipulating spirits to act upon others in harmful ways eventually discover that their helping spirits will leave them. That renders them spiritually defenseless and vulnerable to intrusions and attachments. While the "perfume" of the spiritual power they had gained from helping spirits will linger for a time, eventually the sorcerer will weaken and become subject to harm.

Another ethical concern is how can we know what is truly the right course of action when working with elemental spirits in situations like weather control? We are not likely to have the big picture about how interfering with our weather climate will impact the whole network of ecological relationships. For instance, if a shamanic practitioner works with a nature spirit to induce rain during a drought, what can be the unconsidered effects on the region? Any approach to such interventions should be done with humility and discernment after seeking broad consultations. The shamanic practitioner's best first course of action could be to ask guidance from helping spirits about how she or he can personally respond to the situation (whether in nonordinary or ordinary reality).

Shamanic practitioners need to be vigilant to the temptation to accumulate power for its own sake—resulting in ego inflation and self-aggrandizement. When the primary focus is on gathering power and spirit allies as the measure of our greatness and importance we fail to honor the true responsibility and calling that comes with shamanic work. Shamanic practitioners are in the service of the community by working with spirits for the purpose of bringing healing, wisdom, and knowledge into our ordinary reality.[2]

PRACTICES FOR HEALING AND DIVINATION

It is our contention that spirits affect our spiritual, emotional, mental, social, and physical well-being as humans (as well as other species in this Middle World). Some spirits are benevolent and might even serve as agents of divine desire for supporting wholeness. Others can be harmful to us. We will look at some of the ways shamanic practitioners work with helping spirits for healing purposes. As will be mentioned at other times in this book, there are various ways "healing" can occur. Not all healing results in physical cure and the spiritual healing that a shamanic practitioner works to bring about is not intended to replace the benefits of Western medical practices. Shamanic healing practices (like Christian spiritual healing practices I will discuss in a later chapter) are intended to be complementary to Western medical practices. As with Western medicine, some conditions may require repeated sessions and a period of days following a session before the benefits of shamanic healing are noticed. Sometimes healing is not able to happen in a way we can recognize, whether in shamanic work, Christian spiritual healing, or in Western medicine. There are limits to our understanding and abilities, and sometimes the limits involve the client's ability to respond or life lessons that need to be worked through. Humility in the face of mystery and destiny is an appropriate human attitude in this Middle World.

The following are brief descriptions of shamanic practices that are typically offered as spiritual resources for healing and well-being. The terms and methods that are described may differ slightly depending on how the practitioner was trained and their learning gets refined from their spirit teachers and helping spirits. I want to emphasize that the shamanic practices described here should not be attempted unless you are receiving instruction and supervision through a competent shamanic training organization or are under the guidance and instruction of an experienced shamanic practitioner who has received advanced training. My purpose in this chapter, and later, is to make you aware of the range of shamanic practices for healing and understanding and how Upper and Lower World spirits can assist us.

Guardian Spirit Retrieval. In the shamanic perspective, we humans are given from our birth a helping spirit, and we need this spirit as our ally in defending us in the rough and tumble of Middle World living. Without such a helping spirit (Christians might use the term "guardian angel") we are very vulnerable and subject to sickness and various kinds of spirit attacks that can drain our vitality and cause harm. However, sometimes we may lose our helping spirit. We might feel "dispirited" or chronically depressed or lack vitality, or suffer from a chronic illness that is not responsive to normal medical treatment. The shamanic practitioner will, after consulting with spirit helpers to confirm the course of action, make a shamanic journey to perform a guardian spirit retrieval. Although not restricted to the Lower World or only for animal spirits, the purpose of the traditional journey is to locate a power animal that consents to be a helping spirit for the client and bring it to the client. Once a guardian spirit is retrieved the shamanic practitioner will suggest ways the client can develop a relationship with the spirit if this is unfamiliar to the client.

The client can decide that the particular helping spirit is not a good match and may decline accepting the guardian spirit. Since helping spirits from the Lower or Upper World are highly evolved compassionate spirits that don't get caught up in ego satisfaction they do not get upset if their offer to help a particular person is refused.

Guardian spirit retrievals are also a common part of a broader treatment plan for some other conditions that we'll describe later. Further, guardian spirit retrievals are also offered for people who wish more spiritual power and vitality. We can have more than one spirit ally that works with us in our life. However, it is important to avoid egoic temptations to try accumulating helping spirits as a measure of our power and prestige.

Intrusive Spirit Extraction. In the shamanic experience there are low level spirits in the Middle World that can attach to people and cause localized harm and pain. Sometimes the spirits are just picked up like parasites or the sticky seeds of weeds. Sometimes the spirits are negative and nasty thought forms that are aimed at us by an angry person. The phrase "shooting daggers" comes to mind as an apt descriptor of thought forms that become intrusive spirits. They too can stick to us and work insidiously. Sometimes the intrusive spirit can be the result of a spell cast on a victim. We are most vulnerable to intrusive spirits when we are weak due to stress or low on energy or our defense system is otherwise compromised. The physical manifestation is usually known as pain or a problem with a particular part of the body. It is resistant or slow to respond to usual medical treatment.

The shamanic practitioner, upon confirming this spiritual treatment with the advice of the helping spirits, will enter into a trance and merge with a power animal or other helping spirit. With the aid of the helping spirit the practitioner will be able to "see" the intrusive spirit and remove it. Then the practitioner will clean the afflicted area and seal it for protection.

Soul Retrieval. When we experience trauma, a part of our soul —our spiritual essence—might split off and reside apart from and inaccessible to the sufferer. Most of us have had some soul loss due to the situations that life brings: frightening situations, accidental injuries, chronic illness, and abusive situations can all bring on soul loss. There can be multiple soul fragments that have split off from the body over time due to various traumas. The severity of soul loss can be experienced on a continuum from feeling "dispirited," or feeling like "I've lost a piece of my self," to being "unable to enjoy something that once was a part of me," to coma (nearly complete soul loss), or death (complete soul loss). In soul retrieval the shamanic practitioner journeys into the nonordinary Middle World in search of the soul fragment or fragments that the client desires to have reunited. Upon finding the soul fragment the practitioner seeks the consent of the fragment to come back to the client. If consent is given the practitioner returns the soul part back to the client.

Psychopomp. The word psychopomp is of Greek derivation and means "guide of souls" and refers to guiding the souls of deceased humans to the afterlife. When some humans die under traumatic circumstances their spirit remains stuck in the Middle World. Victims of war, violent accidental death, great fear of punishment, shame, and feelings of unworthiness are some of the conditions that may cause a dead human spirit to remain in the Middle World. Without help, they are unable to move on to the next stage of their life. Some are disoriented and fearful and show the symptoms of being in distress. These suffering human spirits may not even be aware that they are dead. Religions may have rituals that aim to assist souls in moving from this world to the next.

The shamanic practitioner may be trained in psychopomp work to provide compassionate assistance, with the aid of helping spirits, in conducting the souls of the dead to their next destination. In a shamanic journey the practitioner is guided to the suffering human spirit and engages in a conversation to assure that it knows that it is dead. Once that is established the practitioner asks the spirit if it desires to move on to the next world. If consent is given the practitioner will use one of the methods to guide the spirit to that destination.

Not all deceased human spirits are ready to give consent to move on to their next world. Some may choose to remain in this Middle World existence to assist living family or for other purposes. Or it may have something that yet needs to be resolved before the spirit feels free to move on. The basic question is: are you happy here or do you want to move on? If the human spirit is ready to move on it may choose to go to the Upper or Lower World. Those who are strongly influenced by Western orientations and monotheistic religions are likely to choose the Upper World as their destination. Those strongly influenced by nature-based religions and indigenous cultures are more likely to choose the Lower World as their destination.

Compassionate Depossession. Middle World spirits may influence, afflict, or possess a person. Religions may have rituals and methods for dealing with such situations. Christianity has developed "deliverance" practices for freeing victims of spirit influence and affliction, and may employ exorcism rituals for dealing with cases of involuntary possession. Those practices focus on delivering the suffering victim of possession or affliction, but are not concerned about the spirit which is also suffering.

The approach that shamanic practitioners use is remarkably compassionate in that it aims to free both the suffering client and the suffering spirit. It also recognizes that to simply cast away a spirit is less effective than working for the spirit's own release from its suffering. Most such spirits will just find someone else to afflict or possess unless they are also treated.

The shamanic practitioner will also determine the nature of the spirit that is doing the attaching or afflicting. Is it human or some other form of spirit? In shamanic experience many of the spirits are deceased humans who are needing psychopomp help! In their stuck condition in the nonordinary Middle World these suffering human spirits have been attracted to a living human and seek an attachment. The human might have died as an addict or have some other severe condition it suffered with, and it may carry that over to the living human to whom it attaches. The human then develops the symptom the spirit has brought.

There are spirits not of human origin that can afflict a human. Some may simply be in the wrong place or have a legitimate need that it wants recognized and met. Some are "thought forms" that have taken on a life of sorts and need to be removed. Some are very dark and powerful spirits—what we might call demons. But even these spirits are ultimately suffering, since they are caught in an existence controlled by fear and domination and without love and light.

The practitioner opens up communication, with the aid and protection of one or more powerful helping spirits, to work with the afflicting spirit or spirits and also to honor the needs and concerns of the client. The initial purpose is to protect the client and communicate with the spirit to get it to realize that it is wrong to attach to a living human without the human's consent. Then the practitioner engages the spirit in a firm but caring style with the goal of getting it to not only realize its own suffering, but realize also that a path to its own release and true well-being is available. If it absolutely refuses help, it can be isolated in a holding place where it may have the opportunity to eventually move toward the light. It is removed from the client and taken to an appropriate place. The client is then free and if damage is present the helping spirit will work to heal and cleanse the client.

Often the afflicting spirit, upon realizing its own path of healing and freedom, is asked to repair any damage it has made to the client just prior to being given over to helping spirits that take it to its appropriate place for the next stage of its life. Sometimes the spirit makes earnest apologies to the client for the harm it has caused once it owns up to the damage it has done and is ready to leave.

DIVINATION PRACTICES

Shamanic practices also include various ways of receiving knowledge and wisdom from the spirit worlds. Often this is in response to a question the practitioner wants addressed for her/himself or on behalf of another person or group. I mentioned earlier that in hunting and gathering cultures the shaman would seek from the spirits knowledge of where herds of prey were located and when the best time for a hunt might be. The shaman would learn from a plant's spirit the ways it could be used as medicine or food. Since trees and rocks (like all creation from an animist perspective) have a spirit, the shamanic practitioner can seek the counsel of a tree's or rock's spirit about a question or situation and receive images or words or thoughts that can provide guidance. In Luke's gospel, Jesus tells hearers, "I tell you, if these [people] were silent, the stones would shout out" (19:40). He may well be speaking figuratively but he could also be saying something obvious to a first-century culture oriented to shamanic possibilities.

One of my own practices has been to get to know some of the elementals and other spirits in nature in the region where I live. Since I have a daily walk routine (accompanied by some of my spirit friends) on a trail along the San Pablo Bay I have introduced myself to some of the local spirits. The Spirit of the Land has come to me as a large dynamic bundle of earth and stone. I've given it assurances of my appreciation for the beauty and well-being of the region. It has permitted me to journey deep beyond the ground surface and allowed me to observe its ancient structures and forces. I can draw strength and stability from its presence. In my walks I often find Brother Wind stirring and give thanks for its cleansing and enlivening sweeps—and associate it with the Holy Spirit blowing where it will. I've sat on a bench and seen the spirit of the bay come to me, first appearing as a large and dynamic bundle of water but then forming the shape of an elegant woman: the Lady of the Bay. Mount Tamalpais is the largest of the coastal mountains I can see from my house and on my walks on the bay trail. I make shamanic journeys to cultivate my relationship with the majestic and strong spirit of Mount Tam. Likewise, in being spiritually open and present to the beautiful little hummingbird perched on a tree branch near the bench where I sit I can encounter the spirit Hummingbird. These spirit beings can become teachers and companions, enriching our lives and calling us to care for the world around us with greater depth than before. Often along my walks on the trail I simply say a heartfelt greeting to these physical elements and life forms and their embodied spirits who are becoming my friends.

The shamanic journey to visit with a spirit teacher will provide an opportunity to receive knowledge or wisdom about a matter of concern. Likewise, a shamanic divination journey to a power animal about a question or concern will likely result in a response that can illuminate the situation. The "answer" may be given directly or in symbolic actions or metaphoric images, but it will be designed to address the questioner's situation. Sometimes the response will point to an inadequate framing of the question, or indicate that there is something deeper to address than what the initial question posed.

Shamanic practitioners can also make exploratory journeys into the vastness of the Middle World cosmos, as well as explore the different levels of the Upper and Lower World. Journeys made into all of these realms expand the practitioner's perceptions of reality and bring with it a powerful sense of wonder and awe. Shamanic journeying opens our horizon of reality and helps us realize how privileged we humans are to have a small but valued part in the immensity of these worlds. Engaging the compassionate helping spirits of the Upper and Lower World properly evokes humility as we recognize the generous gift of friendship with such wonderful beings.

TRAGIC TENSIONS

In John Mabry's chapter we will see ways where Christianity shares visionary elements that bear a striking resemblance to shamanistic journeys. Since shamanism is likely the spiritual forerunner and foundation of the major world religions it is not surprising that this parallel is present. It is our contention that a respectful relationship between Christianity and shamanism should exist that allows for the gifts that can enrich each tradition.

However, it is extremely important to recognize that the combined might of the Roman Empire and post-Constantinian Christian religious power has, over the centuries, destroyed Western European shamanic cultures and has often oppressed and devastated indigenous shamanism. This militant and triumphalist form of Christianity has allowed no room for other expressions of the human spirit or experiences of spiritual reality. As a Christian this is a bitter and tragic legacy of my religious tradition that must be confronted and offered for repentance. Sadly, this is not just a horrific thing of the past. Michael Harner wrote of Sami (formerly "Lapp") shamans in the past needing to hide their drums in remote locations and only using them in secret:

In northern Sweden in 1983...my wife, Sandra, I and some Sami friends visited a few rural Sami households. I carried my drum in a case. A Lutheran priest followed us from house to house and questioned the people after we left to find out what we were doing with our drum. I found similar Episcopalian missionary pressure a few years later among the inland Inuit in Canada, forcing people to abandon the shaman's drum. As had been the situation for centuries elsewhere, the noise of the drum for journeying made shamans an easy target for identification and retribution.[3]

But even recently persecutions continue. My own religious denomination, Episcopal Church USA, is a liberal church that prides itself on openness to a wide spectrum of theological opinion. But lines have been drawn by some bishops as to what forms of leadership in other faith traditions can be tolerated for Episcopal clergy. And in recent years an Episcopal priest who was elected bishop by the convention of the Diocese of Northern Michigan failed to get the church-wide consent of bishops and standing committees necessary to be consecrated. The problem was reported to center on his advocacy and personal spiritual practice of some Buddhist forms of meditation.

Lillie Fowley Roden, D.Min. is a lay Episcopalian in Texas, a Eucharistic minister; and a retired educator, psychotherapist, and spiritual director. She is also a Pipe Carrier in Earthtribe. Her book *Christianity and Nature-based Spirituality: A Shamanic Journey Through the Medicine Wheel* is a deeply researched study and a wise and integrative exploration of healing and wholeness. She remains rooted in her church but wrote about the difficulty she experienced in the past as she was being considered for ordination:

My journey into the nature-based pathway resulted in conflicts with my primary family and a few members of my traditional church. Some years back, I was sent up for the Episcopal priesthood for the third time and went through the entire process, which is lengthy and difficult. At the last meeting with the Commission on Ministry, the process seemingly ended because I carry a Pipe and claim my nature-based spirituality and honor my genetic lineage.[4]

I write this while holding a great love and appreciation for the Christian faith, especially in its progressive, inclusive, and sacramental aspects. However it is crucial for followers of Jesus to take very seriously the ways that the liberating and healing gospel good news can be betrayed by fear of the other and the lure of power and control. Institutions are just as susceptible as individuals to sins of pride, greed, wrath, and the like. And so the Christian religion under leaders that have succumbed to such distortions has done terrible things in the name of the Prince of Peace. Doing so betrays the spirit of this great tradition.

My purpose in writing this sober recognition of our painful failures as a religion is to acknowledge the harm but not disassociate from the Church. We need to learn from our failings and embrace a broader sense of spiritual belonging. For much good, much healing and wisdom, comes from the community of the followers of Jesus.

2

THE VISIONARY & SHAMANISTIC IN CHRISTIANITY

JOHN R. MABRY

*I*n his second letter to the Christians at Corinth, Paul says something that has stumped people ever since: "I know a person in Christ who fourteen years ago was caught up to the third heaven—whether in the body or out of the body I do not know, God knows. And I know that such a person... was caught up into Paradise and heard things that are not to be told, that no mortal is permitted to repeat."

Most scholars agree that this is Paul talking about himself in the third person, which is not unusual for a person of such robust ego as Paul. What might seem extraordinary to us, however, is that this is a very early testimony to the kinds of experiences we refer to as "visionary," "revelatory," or even "shamanic." But in fact it is not extraordinary at all, because the Christian tradition has never been a stranger to such experiences—they can be found in every tradition of the church, in every age.

This is precisely the kind of "superstition" that our allegedly "enlightened" theologians have been trying to rid us of, especially since the 19th century. In many ways, this has been a laudable project. The historical-critical method of reading scripture has been a great blessing to biblical scholarship, Copernicus and Galileo were on to something, gravity is real, and Darwin tells us more about our actual ancestors than Genesis does.

But...and it's a pretty big *but*...we have lost something precious in the meantime. Liberal and even moderate Christians have accepted the scientific worldview as our default reality, and while that works well for navigating physical space, it does not serve us well in the realm of the Spirit.

Because we have handed over our view of reality—once more, uncritically—to a ready-made paradigm (trustworthy, because "scientific") we have betrayed our tradition and bought into a "lowest common denominator" version of the universe. Henry Corbin called this a Western "agnostic reflex."[1] Instead, I believe we should be saying, like Hamlet, "There are more things in heaven and earth, Horatio, than are dreamt of in your philosophy."[2]

Our ancestors had a mythic mindset. The events of their world took place on multiple levels of reality—both physical and spiritual—creating a rich cosmic environment. By comparison, the scientific worldview we live in is impoverished. The scientific worldview insists that only things that happen on the physical plane are real (and even then, only those things that are measurable and repeatable). If it isn't happening physically, it isn't actually happening. This is a bit like saying, "I have a house with seven rooms in it—but if something isn't happening in my living room, it isn't happening at all."

What the study and practice of shamanism has taught me—as a Christian, clergyperson, and theologian—is that we have been too hasty in resigning the visionary aspects of our faith to the "superstition" dustbin. Such experiences may not belong in the living room, but they do belong in a room of their own—perhaps a chapel—and that room needs to be studied, honored, and explored.

Taking shamanism seriously teaches us that real things happen that are not physical. There is more going on—really going on—than what is confined to our living room. Real things are happening in the chapel, too. Not physical things, but real things just the same. The revered philosopher and Islamicist Henry Corbin called this the *mundus imaginalis*, which he describes as

---

...a world that is ontologically as real as the world of the senses and that of the intellect. This world requires its own faculty of perception, namely imaginative power, a faculty with a cognitive function, a noetic value which is as real as that of sense perception or intellectual intuition.[3]

Corbin coined the term "imaginal" precisely to distinguish it from the fictional connotations of "imaginary" and in his own time he fought against the rational reductionism of the religious imagination of many traditions, especially Islam.

For those of us who live inside the Christian story, we are under constant pressure, even from well-meaning co-religionists, to assign the virgin birth, Jesus' miracles, the Transfiguration, the Resurrection, the Harrowing of Hell, and the Ascension to the category of "myth" (another maligned concept) or "legend" or "superstition." But might we not reclaim some of the truth, power, and glory of our faith if we gave ourselves permission to see them as real events once more? Not physical events, perhaps, but real nevertheless—events that happened in the other room, in the *mundus imaginalis*. Corbin calls the imaginal body "the body of resurrection" to suggest precisely this kind of interpretation.

Such an understanding restores a transcendent, vertical dimension to progressive Christian faith, which has become anemically horizontal and rationalistic, its last-gasp attempt at relevance being a social justice movement with a thin veneer of religious imagery sprinkled on top. There's nothing wrong with social justice, of course, but even Christian efforts at equality and change can be infinitely more powerful if we can connect to a real—if non-physical—presence that supports us, energizes us, inspires us, and incorporates us into itself. Academics call this "mysticism"—a distancing term if there ever was one—but aboriginal peoples just call it "the world we live in."

It *is* the world we live in, of course. We've simply allowed ourselves to be convinced to walk through it with one eye closed. Effective discernment (and basic navigation) would be infinitely aided by binocular vision—both the physical world and the spiritual world have wisdom to offer. We do ourselves— and our faith—a great disservice if we ignore or deny the spiritual reality that is all around us, interpenetrating us, supporting us, and transforming us.

In the apocryphal Gospel of Thomas, Jesus says, "When you make an eye in the place of an eye and a hand in the place of a hand...then you will enter the Kingdom." What this says to me is that we cannot use the eye that we were handed by others, we must fashion our own way of seeing. We cannot use the hand given to us by our parents or ancestors, even our ancestors in the faith. We must fashion a hand that can grapple all that we need grasped now, in our own time. We cannot uncritically accept the mythic worldview our medieval ancestors held, nor should we uncritically accept the scientific worldview currently *en vogue* in contemporary Christianity. Instead, we must fashion a new way of seeing, a new way of handling things—one that acknowledges the truth of the living room as well as the truth of the chapel.

THE MYTHIC OTHERWORLDVIEW

So, when we enter the chapel, what do we find? We find things that the scientific worldview says are impossible...and we are invited to take those things seriously. For while the scientific worldview offers us facts (and I'm not knocking the importance of facts) the mythic worldview offers us something a bit more rarified: wisdom.

Few of the things we find in the chapel will meet the living room criteria of fact-based, historical reality. But that's kind of the point of the chapel. It offers meaning. When Marcus Borg said, "Everything in the Bible is true, and some of it actually happened," he was pointing directly to the difference between these two worldviews. The Bible presents a mythic worldview, one that favors wisdom over history. In this, the Bible is in alignment with many of the native traditions the prophets often malign within its pages. For like the mythic religious wisdom of all faith traditions, what is important here are the stories that provide meaning for our lives, help us navigate the trickier aspects of being human and living in human community, and provide hope for our futures—both individual and collective.

How do we gain this wisdom? For a beginning, it is enough to allow it its place. This is no small feat under the cultural tyranny of the scientific worldview. Just to open a crack to the mythic worldview, to allow it the benefit of a doubt, is tantamount to treason for many. But once we do, once we open ourselves to it and learn to speak its language—a very different sort of language than is spoken in the science-based living room, filled with heroes and symbols and metaphors, where nobody says exactly what they mean and everything points to something else—we discover hidden treasure. It is a treasure that is hard to live without once we find it.

Once we become fluent in its language, its meaning and import grows. It becomes reliable in ways we could not have predicted when we only lived in the living room. We begin to trust it, and the more we trust it, the deeper into it we go. Are we still supported? Yes. Even deeper in, then.

Some remain dabblers in this world, some become inhabitants, and some of us become specialists and professionals. This is the shaman, the priest, the rabbi, the roshi, the imam. Generally, specialists do not self-select—there is a spiritual reality that chooses them and calls them. That spiritual reality goes by many names. It isn't given much love out in the living room, but in the chapel it is the personality and the power behind the myths and symbols and metaphors.

In most native traditions, the shaman is the one the community looks to when something gets out of balance. When the body is out of balance, there is illness; when the community is out of balance, there is conflict; when humans and nature are out of balance, both suffer and often people and creatures die. The shaman's role is to restore balance, and he or she does this by going into the Otherworld to seek wisdom. The Otherworld has a different name in every system, but we'll just say "Otherworld" to keep it generic.[4]

The means of accessing the Otherworld differs from tradition to tradition. For some, it will be drumming or dancing that will allow the shaman to slip across the threshold from our world into another. Some traditions use hallucinogens, while others use meditation or trance-inducing forms of prayer. Anything that can help someone achieve an altered state of consciousness can do it.

These states are not recreational, they are medicinal, because the shaman goes into the Otherworld—often at great personal risk and cost—to seek and retrieve the medicine that will restore harmony to the individual, the community, or to nature. The medicine is seldom an actual herb or drug—it is usually knowledge, or more accurately, *wisdom*.

What's it like in the Otherworld? This differs from tradition to tradition, too. Usually there are several "levels" of experience. An Upper World may be full of light, an ethereal place where the shaman will encounter ancestors and famous people from history. The shaman can talk to them and seek their advice.

A Middle World is often similar to our own, but the moral and spiritual ambiguity and even the brokenness of the place may be more obvious. This is the realm of dangerous spirits and trickster deities. They are there in normal waking life as well, but in the Middle World, one can see them and talk to them. They are no more trustworthy for all of that, however.

Finally, there is a Lower World, a chthonic realm where the goodness of the earth, of nature, is personified and encountered. This is the realm of power animals and creatures of stone, mountain, and tree. This is the root place of reality, and it is from here that energy and power rise up for the healing of all things.

No one makes a shamanic journey for the fun of it. It is serious business. The living room dwellers may scowl, saying that shamanic journeys are "just made up," that they're "all in the mind," or "figments of people's imaginations."

And that very well could be. But that leaves us with a very important question: Does the fact that an experience arises from the imagination discount it? Or, might we say with Henry Corbin, "Spiritual imagination is indeed a cognitive power, an organ of true knowledge?"[5] I will grant you that the imagination tells us little about the facts of the living room, but could it be that the imagination gives us access to the wisdom of the chapel?

This is a matter of faith, of course, and of faith's twin sister, trust. As poet Ralph Hodgson put it, it is "a place that has to be believed to be seen."[6] For people who have never accessed or experienced the chapel, it seems like nonsense. But for those who speak its language, who have found its wisdom trustworthy, that faith comes much more easily.

THE CHRISTIAN OTHERWORLD

Christians don't speak of an "Otherworld" the way Australian Aborigines speak of "The Dreamtime," Celts speak of "Faerie," and other native peoples speak of their respective Otherworlds, but we Christians certainly are possessed of a rich metaphysical landscape that differs from ordinary, waking reality. In this next section we'll explore the sources pointing to this Christian Otherworld, its geography, and its inhabitants.

Scripture. The most important source, naturally, is the Bible itself. From the Jewish scriptures (what Christians call the Old Testament) we are given many shamanic images. The Psalmist summarizes some of these when he sings, "If I ascend to heaven, you are there; if I make my bed in Sheol, you are there" (Psalm 139:8). And Ezekiel gives us an account of an otherworldly vision when he describes the "wheels within wheels" (Ez. 1).

It is in the New Testament that we learn of Satan's fall from heaven (Luke 10:18). Both Mark and Matthew tell us that it's better to pluck out one eye than to enter hell with two (Mk 9:47, Mat 5:29). Peter relates a vision given to him on Cornelius' roof (Acts 10). Paul tells us about a man (himself) rising into the third heaven, and the Revelation of St. John is a feast of otherworldly imagery all by itself. These are all visionary or shamanistic experiences. A main feature of many shamanic journeys is the dismemberment of the journeyer and his/her eventual reconstitution—a fine way of describing crucifixion and resurrection, accounts of which are found in all four gospels.

Apocryphal & Apocalyptic Literature. But the Bible is just the beginning. It is the springboard, but the Christian imagination has gone much further, into much wilder territories than the scriptures themselves have ventured. The apocryphal gospels and acts feature more talking animals, dramatic healings, and more capricious motivations for some of our heroes than the scriptures. The Gospel of Nicodemus, for instance, gives an account of a very shamanic journey indeed as it recounts Jesus' adventures in Hell following the crucifixion and before the resurrection.

Apocalyptic literature may have had its start in the Zoroastrian faith, but flourished in the Jewish and Christian traditions as well. "Apocalypse" is derived from a Greek word that means "to reveal," a very shamanic enterprise. There are two main types of apocalypses—those that predict the events surrounding the end of time and those that reveal the secrets of the Otherworld. This latter variety is less well-known but still quite common, in which we follow a hero of the faith (often a biblical character) on a journey where the secrets of the universe are revealed to him (it's usually a "him"). For instance, in one of the many books attributed to Enoch, we see Enoch journey into Heaven, where he learns the names and functions of the seven archangels, learns that the stars are fallen angels, then descends into Hell and the underworld ("The Book of the Watchers").

The Christian Mystics. While apocryphal and apocalyptic literature can be dismissed as "pious fiction" (and often has been), Christian tradition is filled with people who have had genuine visionary experiences, too. Mechtilde of Magdeburg writes that Jesus,

---

"...took her in his divine arms...in the kiss she was drawn up to the most sublime heights above all the angel choirs. The least truth that I saw and heard and understood there was incomparably more than the loftiest wisdom ever uttered here on earth. I saw there things never heard before, my confessors tell me, for I am ignorant of reading or writing. And now I fear God if I keep silent, but I fear uncomprehending people if I write."[7]

Is Mechtilde writing fiction, or is she relating something she genuinely observed in a vision? Even most scholars would admit the latter.

Likewise, when Julian of Norwich was shuddering in her fever, the crucifix held aloft before her face came to life and began to speak to her. One could dismiss this as a hallucination born of illness, except that the revelations given to her in that experience formed the basis of her writing for the next twenty years, and is one of the most splendid and powerful works of mystical literature in the English language.[8] The fever might have helped Julian cross into the Otherworld, but the medicine she found there, and brought back with her, continues to heal people even today.

Dante Alighieri. Perhaps the greatest work of "shamanistic" literature in the Christian tradition is Dante's *Divine Comedy*, which is an extended apocalyptic work of the revelatory variety. It is clearly, self-consciously fiction, but its form is explicitly shamanistic in that the journeyer embarks because of imbalance and disharmony in his own life, crosses into the Otherworld, journeying through the underworld of Hell, the middle world of Purgatory, and the upper world of Paradise, aided by shamanic guides (Virgil and Beatrice), gathering medicine along the way which he then imparts to those on earth for their edification and healing.

St. Ignatius of Loyola. While many saints and mystics have given detailed instructions for mystical prayer—prayer that ushered one into the Otherworld and back again—it wasn't until St. Ignatius began training spiritual directors and designing spiritual retreats that such experiences were taken out of the specialized confines of the convent and the monastery. In Ignatius' *Spiritual Exercises*, laypeople were invited to participate in mystical prayer, prayer that allowed them access to visionary experiences, and then supported them as they unpacked those experiences later with the aid of a spiritual director for their own spiritual nurture and growth.

The prayer form employed by St. Ignatius asked participants to enter into an experience of what we might call "active imagination" today.[9] He asked them to vividly imagine a particular scene from the gospels, and to pay attention to the details that are not found in the text. For instance: Yes, here is Jesus walking on water—but what does the sea smell like? What are the frightened disciples in the boat saying? What is the pray-er feeling, sensing, thinking?

This form of imaginal prayer is indistinguishable from a shamanic journey, as the things one sees and hears are beyond the control of the pray-er, and the experience must be carefully discerned afterwards for the spiritual wisdom and "medicine" it contains.

The Inklings. Also deeply impactful, yet often unacknowledged, is the twentieth-century contribution of the Inklings and their mythopoetic project to the Christian tradition. The Inklings were an informal literary society of (mostly) Christian academics and fantasy writers, the most significant of them being J.R.R. Tolkien, C.S. Lewis, and Charles Williams. Influenced in equal parts by pre-Christian mythologies (especially Norse), Dante, and Wagner's Ring cycle, the Inklings' shared project was to re-present the Christian mysteries through "mythopoesy" or imaginative means (fantasy).

There are deeply shamanistic elements in the writings of all three Inklings, and all three suggest that the Otherworld is actually more real than consensus reality. In fact, in the writings of the Inklings, our world is simply a dim reflection of the Otherworld, which is by far the more substantial reality. Lewis' short story, "The Shoddy Lands," for instance, depicts a professor "crossing over" into the daily experience of another, and recognizing how fuzzy and inconsequential her daily reality is compared with the Real. This is a theme Lewis explores further in both the Narnia stories and in his novel *The Great Divorce*.

Tolkien depicts a kind of shamanic journey in his short story, "Leaf by Niggle," revealing in his own way the splendid Real and the shadowy reflection of it we settle for in daily life, as well as his own version of a journey through Purgatory.

Finally, Charles Williams' novels are filled with more visionary and shamanistic elements than we can reasonably recount—pick one, any of them, and be bowled over by it. *All Hallows' Eve* is especially rich as it depicts the shamanic journey of a newly dead young woman trying to sort out spiritual reality from deeply engrained (and self-centered) habit.

The testimony of these myriad and diverse voices is strong and compelling: there is no shortage of visionary and shamanic experience in the Christian tradition, we have simply not known to label it as such. But as we become more familiar with the shamanic tradition, we will continue to uncover parallels and analogs among the visionary traditions in our own faith. Just as God has never abandoned any people, in any place, at any time, God has not left us without access to the spiritual world or the medicine it offers. In fact, the prophet Joel promises that its benefits are liberally available to all when he says, "I will pour out my spirit upon everyone; your sons and your daughters will prophesy, your old men will dream dreams, and your young men will see visions" (2:28).

GEOGRAPHY OF THE CHRISTIAN OTHERWORLD

The Christian tradition has its own version of the Lower, Middle, and Upper worlds, and plenty of accounts of people who have travelled there. Paul's account of the man who rose to the third heaven (with which we opened this chapter) is perhaps the oldest that can be counted as specifically "Christian" rather than Jewish. These are places which have objective reality of their own, ancient places, existing and visitable in the present moment rather than possessing an exclusively eschatological (future) reality, such as the location of the final judgment.

Heaven. Heaven is the Christian equivalent of the Upper World, and like the shamanistic equivalent, it is seen as a place filled with light and beauty. The Jewish tradition had no mythology of heaven prior to the Babylonian exile. Up until that point, God's abode was on various mountains (thus the name for God, "El Shaddai," Hebrew for "god of the peaks"). The concept of Heaven was a gift from the Zoroastrians (we will see more of these gifts later), but once it gained a foothold in the Jewish imagination, it flourished.

Heaven is the place where God has "his" throne, and while it is not necessarily associated with the destination of righteous souls in Judaism, Christianity certainly came to see it as such. One of the most memorably dramatic descriptions of heaven is found in the "throne room" sequence in Isaiah's sixth chapter:

I saw the Lord sitting upon a throne, high and lifted up; and the train of his robe filled the temple. Above him stood the seraphim. Each had six wings: with two he covered his face, and with two he covered his feet, and with two he flew. And one called to another and said: "Holy, holy, holy is the Lord of hosts; the whole earth is full of his glory!" And the foundations of the thresholds shook at the voice of him who called, and the house was filled with smoke. And I said: "Woe is me! For I am lost; for I am a man of unclean lips, and I dwell in the midst of a people of unclean lips; for my eyes have seen the King, the Lord of hosts!" Then one of the seraphim flew to me, having in his hand a burning coal that he had taken with tongs from the altar. And he touched my mouth and said: "Behold, this has touched

your lips; your guilt is taken away, and your sin atoned for."
And I heard the voice of the Lord saying, "Whom shall I
send, and who will go for us?" Then I said, "Here I am!
Send me" (6:1-8).

Journeys to heaven, and a record of what people saw there,
are legion in the Christian tradition. We have already
mentioned the pseudepigraphal writings such as the Book of
Enoch, which go back nearly to the beginning of the Christian
tradition, and the writings of the mystics, who are often transported to heaven and report on the activity they see there.
Emanuel Swedenborg wrote voluminously about his visionary
journeys to Heaven (and other places as well). And of course,
Dante gives us the most detailed roadmap, if also the most
fanciful and theologically astute.

Hell. Just as famous as Heaven, though perhaps the object of
more fascination, is the Christian (false) equivalent of the Lower
World, Hell. Another bequest of the Zoroastrians, Hell is
unknown to early Jewish tradition (scripture written before the
Babylonian exile speaks only of "Sheol," a shadowy place of the
dead similar to Hades in Greek mythology). After the exile,
however, Hell became an important fixture in Second Temple
Judaism and was handed on to both Christianity and Islam,
where it looms even larger in the imaginations of the faithful.

Unlike the lengthy and glorious depictions of Heaven found
in scripture, however, our ideas of Hell are given short shrift in
the Bible. Jesus speaks metaphorically of the "outer darkness,"
where there is "weeping and gnashing of teeth" (Matt 8:11), and
warns about being cast into Hell with all your limbs, but gives
no description of the real estate there (Mk 9:43). The Bible's
most vivid description comes from the Book of Revelation, but
does not name it as Hell:

But the cowardly, the unbelieving, the vile, the murderers, the sexually immoral, those who practice magic arts, the idolaters and all liars—they will be consigned to the fiery lake of burning sulfur. This is the second death" (21:8).

Detailed descriptions of Hell will have to wait until later in Christian tradition, and there have been some doozies. One of the earliest and most detailed is probably the aforementioned Gospel of Nicodemus. Dante, once more, provides us with a virtual geography of the place. But one of the most vivid (in the imaginations of English speakers) is from John Milton's *Paradise Lost*:

> *A Dungeon horrible, on all sides round*
> *As one great Furnace flam'd, yet from those flames*
> *No light, but rather darkness visible*
> *Serv'd onely to discover sights of woe,*
> *Regions of sorrow, doleful shades, where peace*
> *And rest can never dwell, hope never comes*
> *That comes to all; but torture without end*
> *Still urges, and a fiery Deluge, fed*
> *With ever-burning Sulphur unconsum'd:*
> *Such place Eternal Justice had prepar'd*
> *For those rebellious, here thir Prison ordain'd*
> *In utter darkness, and thir portion set*
> *As far remov'd from God and light of Heav'n*
> *As from the Center thrice to th' utmost Pole.*
> *O how unlike the place from whence they fell (I.60-75)*

Swedenborg also gives us plenty of descriptions of Hell from his travels there (these are not intended to be metaphoric, but actual accounts—see his famous *Heaven and Hell*, published in

1758). St. Teresa of Avila gives us a vivid description in her autobiography (notable for the high number of Lutherans populating it), and many saints have followed suit. And James Joyce's description in *A Portrait of the Artist as a Young Man* is so over-the-top it's parody—but it is lampooning something real: the sadistic delight with which Christians have often vividly imagined Hell, specifically when imagining what God has in store for our enemies.

But such imaginings betray both our tradition and the shamanic way. The shamanistic understanding is that everything in all the worlds is here for harmony, and to restore harmony. If this is true, then Hell is here for our healing. This is counterintuitive and a hard thing to trust, but this is exactly what both Dante and Swedenborg asserted. In both of their imaginal explorations, the doors in Hell only locked from the inside, people always got exactly what they really wanted, and no punishment was permanent.

Purgatory. Also part of the Christian Otherworldly geography is Purgatory, occupying a middle place between Hell and Heaven. While quite vivid in the Catholic imagination, it has never been part of the Eastern Orthodox landscape and has been banished from Protestant maps due to the lack of evidence for it in scripture. Probably the most convincing allusion to it in the New Testament comes from Paul, when he says,

---

For no one can lay any foundation other than the one that has been laid; that foundation is Jesus Christ...for the Day will disclose it, because it will be revealed with fire, and the fire will test what sort of work each has done. If what has been built on the foundation survives, the builder will receive a reward. If the work is burned up, the builder will suffer loss; the builder will be saved, but only as through fire (1 Cor 3:11-15).

Among Protestants, Anglicans are the most kindly disposed toward the doctrine of Purgatory. While still an Anglican rector, John Henry Newman observed in a sermon,

> Even supposing a man of unholy life were suffered to enter heaven, he would not be happy there; so that it would be no mercy to permit him to enter... There is a moral malady which disorders the inward sight and taste; and no man labouring under it is in a condition to enjoy what Scripture calls the fulness of joy in God's presence."[10]

The Anglican Inklings, C.S. Lewis and Charles Williams, would agree with this assessment, and have both written imaginative treatments of "Protestant Purgatory" experiences (see *The Great Divorce* and *All Hallows' Eve*, for a start). As already mentioned, "Leaf by Niggle" by J.R.R. Tolkien is explicitly purgatorial, but as a Roman Catholic, this is less surprising.

Since Purgatory borders Hell at one end, there are parts of it that are very hellish indeed. And since it borders Heaven at the other end, there are parts of it that are very blissful. And there are many gradations in between, much of it not unlike ordinary life on Earth. Once again, Dante gives us the most detailed roadmap, depicting it as a mountain in the southern hemisphere, but imaginative descriptions abound, especially from Roman Catholic saints. As an almost random example, Dutch saint Lidwina of Schiedam wrote,

> Looking around on all sides, she saw what resembled an

immense prison surrounded with walls of a prodigious
height, the blackness of which, together with the
monstrous stones, inspired her with horror. Approaching
this dismal enclosure, she heard a confused noise of
lamenting voices, cries of fury, chains, instruments of
torture, violent blows which the executioners discharged
upon their victims. This noise was such that all the tumult
of the world, in tempest or battle, could bear no
comparison to it.[11]

This is rich terrain—Heaven, Purgatory, and Hell—and well-travelled in Christianity's two-thousand-year history. It is also well documented, especially in the writings of the saints and mystics, and most comprehensively in Dante (a Catholic) and in Swedenborg (a Protestant). The latter two are particularly important.

The Great Cartographers: Dante & Swedenborg. Although Dante was writing fiction, it was fiction that was intentionally theologically informed. And despite its being presented as fiction, it is his work that has been most influential in shaping how the Christian world understands and images the three Otherworlds of our tradition. Even if one has not read Dante, *The Inferno, The Purgatorio,* and *The Paradiso* have so informed and shaped Western thinking on these worlds that it is impossible to escape its influence.

Swedenborg, however, was not writing fiction. He was using active imagination to actively and intentionally explore these spiritual realms. His experience is probably the most explicitly analogous to the shamanistic "project" to be found in the Christian tradition, and is probably the most extensively well-documented. "Being taken to worlds in space," he writes, "does not mean being taken or traveling in bodies, but in spirit. The spirit is guided through varying states of inner life, which appear to him like travels through space."[12]

Swedenborg's descriptions are often dogmatically held as literal truths by conservative Swedenborgians on the one hand, and interpreted in a symbolic, almost Jungian fashion by liberal Swedenborgians on the other. To my knowledge, neither have approached his explorations as shamanic journeys in which he went into the Otherworld and returned with medicine to restore healing and balance to the earth and its inhabitants, but to approach their work in such a way could prove fruitful indeed.

Christians of other stripes have historically dismissed Swedenborg and his journeys out of hand—unfairly, in my estimation. A shamanistic approach here, too, may yield surprising insights with gifts for all Christians. After all, Swedenborg never believed he ought to set up a separate church—he was simply a Swedish Lutheran during his life. He believed his visionary journeys were a gift to the church at large. He needs to be rediscovered beyond exclusively Swedenborgian circles. He needs to be given a fresh hearing. Instead of revering him as a cartographer of literal landscapes or dismissing him as a charlatan, we need a third way—to approach him as a shaman journeying to the Otherworld in search of medicine. Few spiritual explorers in our tradition have amassed such a wealth of wisdom on Heaven and Hell and the purgatorial spaces in between.

INHABITANTS OF THE CHRISTIAN OTHERWORLD

Animals. For good or ill, the Christian Otherworldview is far more anthropocentric than the otherworldviews of native traditions. The Bible mentions a talking donkey and snake (Num 22:30 and Gen 3:1-4, respectively) and the Acts of Thomas has another talking snake...and that's about it for animals in the Christian tradition, historically. That doesn't mean that animals won't speak in your own imaginal prayer, but they're in scarce supply in scripture and tradition.

Humans. That said, there certainly are some fascinating people to encounter. According to the Christian doctrine of the Communion of Saints, all those who have been joined to Jesus in baptism are alive, conscious, and in community with God, with one another, and with us.

That's a lot of people. And all of them are available to talk with us, in imaginal prayer. Do you want to talk with Paul? He's not hard to find, but I warn you, he's still prickly. Want to hear the details of Thecla's story? She's always eager to talk. And of course, Jesus is always available for a heart-to-heart.

Angels. Humans and the occasional talking animal aren't the only creatures in the Christian Otherworldview. Scripture gives ample testimony to spiritual beings, as well—and this prolifer-ates exponentially in the tradition.

In pre-exilic Judaism, angels were few and far between. The word simply means "messenger," and when, on the few occa-sions they appear in early Jewish scripture, they are theophanies —veiled encounters with God. For instance, when Jacob wres-tled the angel in Genesis, he said, "I saw God face to face, and yet my life was spared" (32:30). Other encounters are similar.

But after the exile, the Jews were deeply impressed by the Zoroastrian doctrine of the *spentas*—vast armies of angelic beings of many varieties and occupations—and absorbed the teaching into Judaism, eventually passing it on to Christianity and Islam.

The most dramatic description of angels in scripture are the cherubim, whom Ezekiel describes as God's throne-bearers. Ezekiel speaks about four of them, depicting them with eight wings each, and with very different faces—one has a face like a man, one like a lion, one like an ox and one like an eagle (1:10). They burned like coals and lightning flashed forth from them as they moved. These same creatures also make an appearance in

Isaiah, Daniel, and the Revelation of John, with minor differences in appearance (such as their exact number of wings).

We meet two archangels in scripture—Gabriel and Michael. Gabriel announces to Mary that she is with child in the Gospel of Luke (1:26-38) and Michael argues with Satan in the Epistle of Jude (1:9). The argument apparently escalates, because when we next see Michael, he defeats Satan, casting him from heaven down to the earth (Rev 12:7-12). Two other archangels have prominence in the tradition: Raphael and Uriel. We see Raphael in the apocryphal (aka deutero-canonical) book of Tobit as the mentor and savior of the young hero Tobias. Uriel is also testified to in the apocryphal/deutero-canon, in the apocalypse known as Second Esdras.

But the Christian imagination didn't stop there. In the fourth or fifth century, a writer known as Pseudo-Dionysius produced *On the Celestial Hierarchy* which described vast armies of angels arranged into three broad "spheres" of duty. The first sphere serve the Son of God and include seraphim, cherubim and thrones.[13] The second sphere rule the heavens and the lesser spiritual beings, and their ranks are composed of Dominions, Virtues, and Powers. The third and lowest sphere are those spirits that have contact with human beings: principalities, archangels, guardian angels and generic angels.

Christian writers ever since have been deeply influenced by Pseudo-Dionysius' organizational schema, and although they tweaked it slightly, it survived more or less intact well into the middle ages.

Demons. Another gift of the Zoroastrian tradition to the Abrahamic religions is the evil counterpart to angels—demons. There is the chief demon, of course, Satan himself (also known as Lucifer and Beelzebub) but there are many lesser demonic beings under his influence and command. We meet many of these in the gospels, especially the Gospel of Mark, where Jesus is presented first and foremost as an exorcist. On nearly every page of Mark's gospel, Jesus meets someone who is oppressed or possessed by demons and delivers them, often after a heated exchange with the demon itself (see Mk 1:24).

The demons are vivid characters in the writings of the desert fathers and mothers. These are the folks who fled to the wilderness when the church was granted safety and privilege in the Roman empire because the grand basilicas, elaborate rituals, and backroom influence-peddling among the bishops bore little or no resemblance to the honest and austere faith they had always known. There in the desert they may have been surprised to encounter as many demons as they had fled the cities to get away from. Because Christians compulsively group things into threes, Evagrius the Solitary wrote, "Of the demons opposing us in the practice of the ascetic life, there are three groups who fight in the front line: those entrusted with the appetites of gluttony, those who suggest avaricious thoughts, and those who incite us to seek the esteem of men." It is not accidental that these categories match the temptations of Jesus in Matthew 4:1-11 precisely.

As with all things in the Christian imagination, time brings proliferation. Medieval grimoires and Christian cabalistic writings further categorized varieties of demons, creating "lowerarchies" clearly mirroring the angelic hierarchy of Pseudo-Dionysius. Some of these, such as *The Lesser Key of Solomon*, were arranged for the express purpose of exploiting the demons' power in black magical operations, while others were simply exercises in metaphysical sociology.

When some of my students or parishioners ask me about demons today, I tell them, "There are forces both within us and without us that seek our undoing. You can call them what you like, but 'demons' works just fine for me."

Both angels and demons are firmly rooted in the Christian imagination, and time has not diminished their importance. While there are certainly many Christians that dismiss both out of hand under the rationalistic influence of the living room, angels and demons remain active and populous participants in the spiritual lives of many.

ACCESSING THE OTHERWORLD

Typically, in native traditions, shamans access the Otherworld through trance states induced through drumming or dance or hallucinogenic plant medicine. Christian prayer, too, utilizes trance states in order to "cross over" into the Otherworld. This is certainly done in mystical prayer, which, like many forms of meditation, often takes years of practice to do well. From the Hesychastic prayer of the Orthodox tradition (reciting the "Jesus Prayer" thousands of times in succession) to the medieval manuals on recollection, to the Spiritual Exercises of St. Ignatius, to the more contemporary Centering Prayer, there have always been contemplative prayer practices that can usher the pray-er into the Otherworld. Nor is there any shortage of accounts of what Christians find in that Otherworld. One need only pick up the book of a random Christian mystic to be amazed and inspired by the profundity of their journey.

Liturgy & Eucharist. Less obvious, perhaps, is the way that liturgy can also function to usher worshippers into the Otherworld. Orthodox worship is especially well-suited for this, as it is attempting—as well as is humanly possible on earth—to reproduce and participate in the worship going on in heaven. To step into an Orthodox worship service in full swing—with its glowing candlelight, incense, gold leaf, proliferation of icons, and haunting, otherworldly choir—is to step out of ordinary reality and into the Otherworld itself, a liminal, in-between place (and in-between time) that is not quite this world and not quite Heaven. It is, however, to see Heaven, to taste Heaven, to have it within tantalizing reach. One does not emerge from Orthodox worship bored or distracted, but overwhelmed and exhausted from the constant assault on the senses, a quiet barrage of beauty. One does not find access to the Otherworld in Orthodox worship, it *is* the Otherworld, and one should not be surprised to meet angels and saints while there.

Western liturgy is more austere, but if one can connect theologically to what is being enacted, access to the Otherworld is still possible. For instance, the liturgy of the Eucharist in most Western rites begins with the following preface and Sanctus:

It is right, and a good and joyful thing, always and everywhere to give thanks to you, Father Almighty, Creator of heaven and earth... Therefore we praise you, joining our voices with Angels and Archangels and with all the company of heaven, who forever sing this hymn to proclaim the glory of your Name: Holy, holy, holy Lord, God of power and might, heaven and earth are full of your glory. Hosanna in the highest. Blessed is he who comes in the name of the Lord. Hosanna in the highest.

"Holy, holy, holy" is the liturgy being sung in Heaven (from Isaiah chapter six, which we visited earlier), but what the preface makes clear is that the worship in any given church service (enacted with the small group present, around this physical altar, in this earthly place) is at the same time participating in the heavenly liturgy, and adding our own voices to it. It's kind of an "Act locally, think cosmically," form of worship. Our local worship is part of one great service with the worship in Heaven as well as the worship around every altar in the world, both now and across time. This sense of chronological mysticism is amplified by various strands of the Eucharistic prayer that make it clear that in this rite, the veil is pulled back to make us present at the Last Supper with Jesus, while another strand suggests that the meal allows us to move forward in time, too, making us present at the Feast at the End of Time foretold in Isaiah's vision of the mountain (Isaiah 25:6-8).

We made this explicit in my own congregation by composing the following Presentation of the Gifts to prepare those gathered around the communion table for what they are about to experience:

Raising the bread, the celebrant says: When Jesus gathered with his friends on his last night with them, he blessed bread and broke it. This is the bread that was served at that meal. Let us partake of that bread tonight.

People: Let us be glad and rejoice in God's salvation!

Raising the cup, the celebrant says: At the world's end, God will host a feast of rich food for all peoples, where none will ever be hungry or thirsty again. This is the wine that will be poured at that meal. Let us partake of that wine tonight.

People: Let us be glad and rejoice in God's salvation!

The Eucharist, then, is not just a memorial of the Last Supper, but a portal into the Otherworld. Bread and wine are medicines which are brought back for the healing of all who partake of them. As early as the 2nd century, St. Ignatius of Antioch wrote of the Eucharist, "Breaking one and the same bread, which is the medicine of immortality, and the antidote to prevent us from dying, but that we should live forever in Jesus Christ."[14]

Baptism. Other sacraments are likewise rich. Familiarity with baptism has made us blind to its mystical import, which has led to a dire condition within the church in which even clergy declare it "just" a symbol instead of the profoundly shamanic initiation experience it is—or should be. Baptism is the rite in which a person is mystically united with Jesus—becomes one being with Jesus—and with everyone else who has been united to him as well, past, present, and future. And just as shamans use ordinary physical objects to effect their cures—smoke, sweetgrass, rattles—baptism employs the simple element of water to effect its transformation.

A familiar experience during a shamanic journey is the dismemberment and restoration of the journeyer. Baptism offers its own version of this as the initiate goes down into the water and is drowned in a dramatic reenactment of Jesus' own murder—and then participates in his resurrection as he or she is pulled from the water restored and alive, a transformed, new sort of creature. As Paul writes,

---

Do you not know that all of us who have been baptized into Christ Jesus were baptized into his death? Therefore we have been buried with him by baptism into death, so that, just as Christ was raised from the dead by the glory of the Father, so we too might walk in newness of life (Rom 6:3-4).

This is not mere metaphor as those in the living room would have us believe. This is deep mysticism, profound transformation, and strong medicine not dissimilar to that experienced in shamanic journeys and healings.

WHO MAY ACCESS THE OTHERWORLD?

There was a time when the sacred was just part of everyday life, but as our ideas about the Divine became more complex, our religions did too, and a specialized class of clergy was called forth. The first of these were shamans, but most traditions have their own professionals, including the Christian tradition, with our priests and pastors and vowed religious.

In native traditions, it was the shaman that discerned the need for balance, and the shaman who made the journey into the Otherworld to seek medicine, often at great personal risk to him- or herself. Likewise, it is the priest or pastor who normally performs the sacraments, hears the people's confessions, and guides them in prayer.

But there has been a great democratization of spirituality in the past fifty years. While there are still dedicated shamans, more and more people are going on shamanic journeys of their own under a shaman's guidance, rather than simply having the shaman journey for them. The Otherworld is not only for the professionals—it is a spiritual treasure for all peoples.

Likewise, while in the Christian tradition mystical prayer has long been thought to be the domain of vowed religious, St. Ignatius was leading laypeople in imaginal prayer as far back as the sixteenth century. Many Christians are availing themselves of spiritual directors, the writings of the medieval mystics are now widely available in translation, and hesychastic prayer and Centering Prayer are experiencing wide popularity. When Jesus rightly criticized the Pharisees, saying, "they are like a dog resting on the oxen's manger—it neither eats, nor allows the oxen to eat" (Thomas, 102) he was speaking of a time that would be difficult to go back to, as the "gatekeepers" of spirituality are no longer automatically afforded respect in our culture, but must earn it by being worthy guides who make the mystical treasures of our respective traditions available to all who wish to partake of them.

CONCLUSION

Beyond the scientific worldview there is another reality, arguably more real than our culture gives it credit for. This reality is accessible through the organ of the imagination through mystical prayer and shamanic journeys. It is only through such contact that the healing wisdom of the soul can be discerned, retrieved, and applied for the healing of our spirits, our bodies, our communities, and the world.

Christianity is not a stranger to this medicine. The Epistle to the Hebrews might easily be rewritten to speak of Jesus as the great shaman who journeyed to the underworld and returned for the healing of all peoples, bringing with him medicine that is still healing people today. This is all the more rich with meaning in the Christian tradition if we remember that Jesus is "the wisdom of God" (1 Cor 1:24)—he is both the bringer of medicine and he is himself the medicine.

This fits in well with the medical model of Christianity that views human beings not as morally "depraved," as Calvin would have it, but as sick with a chronic condition that is not our fault, but which nevertheless causes much suffering. Jesus brings the medicine which controls the condition and makes it manageable until the healing of all things is complete.

St. Ephrem of Syria wrote extensively about this medicine, saying,

---

To the palsied [Jesus] granted healing, who arose and walked and carried his bed. And to us he has given the pearls; his holy Body and Blood. He brought his medicines secretly; and with them he heals openly. And he wandered round in the land of Judea, like a physician, bearing his medicines."[15]

In another place, he prays, "Who will cure my soul if not Thou, O Christ, the only Physician of souls! Where will I find a remedy for the disease of my soul, if not with Thee, O fountain of healing!"

This way of viewing Christianity in general and mystical prayer in particular requires more contemplation and study. I hope that this essay and this volume contribute in some small part to the beginning of this exploration. It is my hope that we can begin to see the imagination as an organ of spiritual perception—as Ignatius and Swedenborg did and to preach and teach it, training people in imaginal prayer, and benefitting from the medicine and wisdom they return with.

3

A JOURNEY OF HEALING AND INTEGRATION

KATRINA LEATHERS

*M*y story speaks from the perspective that spirituality and shamanism are deeply integrated with psychology; I see psyche as one multifaceted thing. The practices, beliefs and possible healing that are part of psychological processes and of spirituality are interrelated phenomena, ways of looking at one complex thing.

Shamanic practice most often serves by healing others from physical or spiritual ailments, although the same purpose can be applied for oneself. My experience in this realm ostensibly started as healing of my own psychic wounds, but it was also preparation to bring that work to others. As I describe below, that personal journey was great training for ministry, through a mode I think of as shamanic counseling, or spiritual direction with the spirits.

My lifelong challenge, from my 55-year-old viewpoint, has been to see and trust the presence of Other, on all levels of experience. Disbelief has been the primary obstruction in relationship with the Divine as well as with human beings. In shamanic practice, through journeys and the teachings of spirits, I began to understand the depth of this injury, and to open to the connection that can be, if one allows it, a powerful source of strength and support.

Shamanic work showed me the shapes and the edges of this story in my life. Without feeling the support and comfort of a loving presence of Other, this life felt too difficult. My subconscious urge to leave this earth, to escape, became so clear in my journeys that the appearance of health issues was not a surprise. My body expressed my ambivalence about life through serious illnesses—possible escape avenues and metaphoric manifestations of what my soul was holding. Shamanism gave me the vision to see and the spirit help to transform this story.

This has been my sustained spiritual challenge: How can I connect to Spirit, in any form, if I cannot believe and trust in that presence? How can I live closely with Other if I cannot open to their presence and love? How can I survive without doing exactly those things? Twelve years of shamanic work (in addition to other spiritual and healing pursuits) have been reshaping this paradox at my core. Only the spirit helpers (or maybe a good therapist) would have had the patience to repeatedly offer the same healing, the same teachings, giving over and over what I needed to embrace this human life.

Carl Jung's concept of "the wounded healer" teaches that the wound is the gift, on the path of a person in service to humanity. My prenatal and early childhood injury created the yearning and the need to find my way to Spirit, to learn the ways of that path. Nonordinary reality (NOR) in shamanic practice was where I directly experienced Divine power and presence. That direct connection, the palpable relationship with spirit helpers and teachers, was the path toward belief, mending the distrust and lack of object permanence I carried from early years. The wounds attuned my sensors to seek Divine presence and kept me ferociously on the path to secure that connection which was so hard to hold onto. All of what I experienced early on led me to shamanic work. The shamanic work eventually bound me to earth, ready to help others to ferociously seek their own form of connection to spirit and thus a stronger embrace of this life.

BACKGROUND

From the beginning, spirits were a real and respected presence, alongside God, Baha'ullah, and prophets throughout time. Since I was rooted in the Baha'i faith through childhood, prayer and talking to God were a comforting practice for me in the midst of a chaotic family life. Between Baha'i theology and my mother's mystical bent, Spirit was a palpable presence in prayer, in respect for ghosts, and even through a Ouija board. Witnessing the inexplicable, opening the doorway for spirit to speak through my mother, aunt, friends and myself, created an experiential knowing of the reality of invisible beings sharing our existence. God was, and still is, an omniscient and beneficent presence, but the presence of spirits was much more tangible, accessible, and dynamic.

In addition to that family influence, I was raised mostly in the country and spent long days outdoors, sitting with big rocks at the stream, talking with daffodils and resting in the arms of the oak tree. I curled up at my window at night, watching the stars. The world outside felt rich and full of a mysterious, compelling aliveness.

Coming from that foundation, I walked through this world knowing that we are part of a much bigger reality, surrounded by powers invisible to us. The difficulty for me was finding a way to connect to that, to feel the presence of something I could know as "God." The God who lived way up above was hard for me to reach, so I wandered through my 20s and 30s searching for that elusive deep communion.

BEGINNING: FINDING THE PATH

For me, as for many, it was loss that brought me to the threshold of the shamanic territory. It was deeper crisis that then revealed the power and wisdom of the world of spirits.

The beginning was my move to California, after 42 years on the East Coast. Following a job for my husband-of-the-time, I landed in the urban chaos of Oakland, California, 3,000 miles from home, knowing just two people in the area. My husband disappeared into his job, and I sought solid ground for myself and my two small kids, Mateo and Lucia. In that context, the challenge began with the heart-failure of my beloved Nana, my "good mother," just two weeks after we arrived in California. I spent the next 6 months flying back and forth, California to Maine, to be present for her last months on earth. When she died in September, 2005, I was bereft and fell into over-whelming grief.

Lost in a dark place, I clearly needed help, but I didn't know what that might be. I had trained and worked as a psychotherapist and had also been in therapy myself, so I had plenty of respect for psychological work. However, I knew that work would not bring the light I needed. Divine intervention spoke through my friend Beth: "You should go see Wendy—she's a shaman." I knew nothing about shamanism, but followed the signposts that appeared. In my first meeting with Wendy, she introduced me to shamanism, as she shook a rattle and I journeyed to the lower world. Since that day in December 2005, connecting to Spirit through shamanic practices has been my spiritual home, the place I go for healing, guidance, and teaching. Wendy opened the doorway into nonordinary reality, but my primary teachers were always in and of the spirit world.

FIRST YEARS: ESTABLISHING RELATIONSHIPS

Without any formal training, I dived into journeying, meeting Wendy often and journeying alone in-between. The first two years were full of grace, a delightful discovery of the non-ordinary landscape, rich with relationships with spirit helpers and teachers. My first teacher there was Nana, my grandmother who had recently died. In an early journey, I asked her what she came to teach me, and she replied, "I am here to teach you to fly." Nana led me through the first months of shamanic exploration, pointing me toward further study and practice. When I asked her in a journey about my future work, she carried me to the San Francisco office where Wendy and I met. She and Wendy surrounded me as I journeyed *within* the journey, showing me that my work was in this arena. In a sleeping dream around this same time, Nana again pointed me toward the shamanic path, telling me there was work for me to do in this world and that shamanism was part of it.

While Nana was the first to help me in the realm of spiritual reality, it quickly became clear that my primary teacher was the being who took both human and bird form. Whether as the large black bird or the impatient irreverent man, Raven both talked with me and led me into experiences, over and over, with clear teaching and/or healing content. Over the years, that relationship remained potent, even through times of distance or even struggle. Raven has directed, challenged, occasionally joked and rarely comforted, but always led me forward on the path of spiritual deepening and transformation.

SPIRIT HELPERS, TEACHERS AND PROTECTORS

Other beings began to join me in my journeys, and soon there was a small crew of regulars, each with their own way of being present, with offerings as well as requests for me. Many of them have stayed for years, while others have done their job and moved on. Many have appeared occasionally, or even just once, with a particular purpose or teaching, but have not joined my "central crew."

Eagle was the first to appear after Raven. Many times, I was taken up to Eagle's nest for rest and renewal. Sometimes my children, in spirit form, would be taken there as well and left for safekeeping. Without ever speaking a word, Eagle gave me an awareness of the big picture and a sense of trust, even when much in life seemed tentative. Over the years Eagle became a consistent presence. With Eagle's presence, I was invited to deepen my resilience and trust through whatever might occur.

Lion was another important companion in my first years. While he rarely "spoke" to me, his role clearly was to bring protection against external dangers. Accompaniment by or merger with spirits for protection is a classic part of shamanic work, and his presence was powerfully consistent in a time I needed that. I learned to pay more attention to what was going on when he showed up, as he signaled a potential danger. I became adept at feeling or invoking the power of his presence when a threat (spiritual, emotional, or physical) seemed to be nearby. The critical job of protection during a risky time brought him into my journeys frequently, until that phase ended and his job was complete. After that phase, his help was not needed and he rarely shows up now.

Another one of that first crew was Tiger, bringing courage, strength and vitality. For him and as him, I was asked to dance, to increase those qualities in myself, feeling the spirit of Tiger in me. Merging with him was like a shot of adrenaline, filling me with an energy that was missing before Tiger appeared. Tiger is not a teacher, but a great helper who gives something vital and necessary when I am facing a challenging task.

Sometimes a spirit teacher is just "visiting faculty" who shows up for one brief lesson, often with surprising content. At one point I journeyed to the spirit of a succulent plant that seemed to call me, to ask how to improve my serenity. The spirit of that plant showed up as a feisty warrior in green armor, calling himself "Randy." He took me riding through the sky in his jet ski, and adamantly instructed me to "seize your joy—be fierce," saying that joy would be found through dance and sexuality. Randy has never again appeared, but his message was strong and clear and has stayed with me ever since.

RECIPROCITY AND TRUST

Through the years, I have been asked to do various things to support my shamanic development, or for healing purposes for myself or others. Once a task is given, I am often then given something needed to complete the task; spirits rarely leave me on my own. Early on, I was told to wear symbols of my spirit helpers, to always remember and call in their help. I easily found a silver eagle and a feather to symbolize Raven, as well as a small Elephant, and put them on a chain around my neck. Lion was harder to find, and I searched in vain for a lion to add to my talismans. Given the protection I seemed to need, the absence of Lion's symbol was disconcerting. One day, working in the backyard of our house, I found buried in the dirt a collection of broken pieces of glass with gold stamped on them. One glass piece—a perfect size to wear on a necklace—included the gold footprint of a cat and the words "like a lion." I was given what I needed right in my backyard! I wrapped the glass piece with Lion's symbol in silver wire and wore it around my neck, feeling the tangible presence of the spirits' help.

Through this and many similar incidents of apparent Divine intervention, my trust in Spirit deepened. This growing trust and willingness to surrender to the power of the Divine was an essential piece of my spiritual development. This foundation was built in the first two years of my shamanic work and was preparation for the initiations that were still ahead.

COMMITMENT: THE THREE-YEAR PROGRAM

After the first year of working with Wendy, I began training with Michael and Sandra Harner. After several introductory weekends, I entered the "Three-Year Program of Advanced Initiations in Shamanism and Shamanic Healing" at the Foundation for Shamanic Studies. Twice a year we met for five-day residential retreats, for teaching, group practices, and initiations. During those three years, I still saw Wendy for mentoring, spiritual counseling, and further teaching. Those years would be a full of challenges both internal and external, and shamanic practice was critical through it all.

During this time, the distinction between this work and psychotherapy became clear. From my training as a therapist and my previous internal work, I knew the power of therapeutic processes. In my shamanic studies, I could see that working on the spiritual level of reality, in shamanic experiences, had a different power than that of good psychotherapy. The shamanic healing never seemed to be spiritual bypass, just a different process than healing through psychotherapy. Neither one is a replacement for the other nor a lesser form of transformation; the two are complementary and also synergistic in their impact.

SHAMANIC HEALING ON ALL LEVELS

The different levels of being that we usually perceive and believe in—physical, emotional, spiritual—are not, in spiritual reality, separate and distinct in the way we often *believe* they are in ordinary reality. Healing that occurs may seem to be focused on a physical aspect of being, but this can also be understood as a metaphor, symbolic for something on the spiritual or psychological level. Awareness of the metaphoric nature of what is presented helps in understanding the dimensions of reality behind the metaphor.

My chest has always been an area of focus in journeys, with repeated rituals of being cut open, clearing or removing things held there. Many times, diamonds, malachite, light or other healing forms have been placed inside my chest. My psychic "heart" had been damaged by early trauma and a difficult childhood, and it needed healing. The injury to my psychic heart paralleled the physical manifestation of a heart defect, dangerous bouts of pneumonia, and eventually even worse. My heart was not able to be open and trusting, leading to difficulty in trusting Spirit as well. I was not yet able to surrender into the care and power of Spirit. This interconnected web of challenges and healing of the "heart" needed to be addressed on all levels of my being, from the western medical treatment of the physical to the spiritual and psychological healing through the shamanic approach.

METAPHORS FOR THE JOURNEY

Metaphors are often the means by which by Spirit communicates in both healing and teaching, showing us the reality at hand and possibly the way ahead as well. As with the metaphoric nature of my heart's healing, the metaphors were rich and plentiful in the years of shamanic work that followed.

Steel rods. Early on, Wendy journeyed for me and saw four vertical steel rods in my torso, formed in childhood when I did not feel safe. Wendy reported that removal of these rods would be part of my learning to surrender, to trust and believe that Spirit was with me, that Spirit would in fact *hold me up.* This metaphor of my body being held up by steel rods expressed my emotional, psychological reality, and an aspect of my spiritual being that needed to be "dismembered" and healed.

This journey revealing the steel rods was followed by journeys to the tree spirits Hazel and her sisters Laurel and Willow. With Hazel and her sisters, I often transformed into a small child, being held as they soothed and comforted me. In those journeys, the steel rods were removed by Hazel or by Raven, softening the rigidity in my chest. Part of this healing was simply teaching me to listen to what I felt on each level of my being. Releasing the metaphoric rigidity in my awareness allowed me to connect more deeply to what I experienced in the past and present—a critical skill in this area of work.

Repetition of a process, like the opening of my chest, is how shamanic healing often works, and I would experience spiritual surgery on my heart or chest many times again. Strangely and perfectly affirming the truth of interconnected levels of reality, this was paralleled by physical reality, as I would require multiple (medical) surgeries in my chest area in the years following this shamanic healing ritual.

Fire. Fire was another metaphor prevalent in my early shamanic work, symbolizing that tumultuous time of change. Raven frequently brought me to fires and spoke of hard times ahead with much loss and destruction. At one point, he said I was walking into a fire which would burn off what was not needed. In another journey, he brought me to a burnt forest with brush gone and the earth bare and dark. I was told that fire and all it brings was another way of healing.

TEACHING JOURNEYS

All along the way, we are given golden nuggets of wisdom, teachings about shamanic work, our own path, or just tools for everyday life. At times this may be a simple statement, like a mantra or koan. For example, recently I was told: "You don't need to *know*; you just need to *see*." Other times, it is a longer teaching, often on the nature of shamanic work and how to engage with it for healing of self or others.

One lovely lesson I was given is that just *being with* a spirit helper brings healing and spiritual help, whether in a journey or in ordinary reality with shamanic consciousness (connecting without a "journey"). I learned to connect to particular spirit helpers and their particular gifts or powers. I called in Lion when I felt the need for protection (although he usually just showed up when there seemed to be danger). I would merge with the big evergreen tree for regenerative quiet time. I connected to Tiger for strength, energy, and action when that was needed. I climbed into the lap of Great Spirit Mother when needing comfort or nurturance. Hawk or Eagle would take me flying, maybe resting in some high-up location, to see the big picture and find perspective. I learned to follow Raven to find teachings I needed, and to see my next steps. The spirit helpers often do not *do* anything in particular; they simply bring their own special presence and power. Being with them can give whatever is needed without any explicit healing ritual or teaching.

Another teaching was on the nature of discernment with spirit help. When making a decision, we may seek guidance but still have full responsibility to make the choice. We are not to rely on directives, even from spirits.

As I contemplated my marriage, I asked my spirit teacher: "Can we make this marriage work?" Raven asked if I was willing to follow my individual path, whatever that might bring. He said it was my choice and showed me the two future selves I could become. The path of separation, following my own call, would take me to a darker, deeper, more connected, and powerful way of being. Choosing the option of preserving the marriage was simpler, remaining who I was then: lighter, with more ease, but less satisfied and engaged with life. I was shown the two futures, the two women I could become, and clearly told that I needed to make the choice. For the path I chose, to follow my individual call away from the marriage, I was told that Lion, Tiger, and Raven would be my strength and help. They were companions on that path, but they did not direct my decision to leave. The two visions I was given expanded my understanding, without a judgement as to which path was best for me. The spirit help given was simply more awareness, plus the reminder of my power of choice, not a directive from outside myself.

Spirit's teachings are often repeated messages like these that I received, like signposts along the road:

- Isis often tells me to dance, be in my body, and not be afraid of her power.
- Raven reminds me to open my heart and to listen to more music, to connect to a deeper level of feeling and listening.
- Nana comes to tell me I am loved by Spirit, and that Spirit is always with me.
- Many beings remind me, "Find joy, trust joy, expand joy."

Sometimes, the teachings have a more difficult tone, as they address deeper territories of psyche:

- Raven tells me: "I am the darkness; darkness is your teacher. Do not flee the darkness; embrace it, be in the unknown. The dark is full, rich with treasures you need. Do not be afraid."
- Great Spirit Mother tells me, "You will not be lost forever. You will find your way."
- Isis says: "You have only just begun. You just walked

into the fire and now you need to go through it. Hold
onto your hat and *dance!*"
- Raven says: "After the tears will come something else.
  Don't forget that you can *fly*."

Journeys taken by other practitioners also revealed teachings
and guidance along the way. I ask a friend for input on how to
become stronger for the work I will do in the world. She brings
me this from her helping spirit: *There is a long distraction in the*
way, something yet hidden but big that needs to be dealt with first,
something to do with being a mom and a wife, something about the
feminine that is urgent. There is something you need to know but don't
yet see. There will be letting things go, and endings, and then later
moving into an easier time. I heard this the week I took off my
wedding ring, so I imagined it was about the change in my
family. As always, the vision of Spirit was greater than my own.
I moved blithely into the upheaval of everything without
knowing how big or urgent that would actually be.

MOVING TOWARD CRISIS

After the initial phase of forming strong relationships with my
spirit helpers and peering into my own psychic dark caves, it
came time to grapple with the demons in those caves. The help
and the teachings of spirits would become more crucial than I
yet understood. In this time I began to clearly see the reality and
strength of my ambivalence about being alive, and the dangers
of holding that feeling. A series of journeys, described below,
helped me to see and shift that ambivalence, and get both feet
planted on this earth.

In August 2006, I was instructed to journey to meet with
someone who had who died years ago. The spirit of Emily
Dickinson apparently had something important to tell me, as I
could not think of *anyone* dead except her! My teacher lead me

into the journey and we found her spirit in a tight, dark, crowded space. In that space with her, I sensed no movement, nothing alive or vibrant in any way. Merging with her consciousness, my body ached and itched all over. I felt constricted, trapped, and wanted to scream and escape. I felt a powerful remorse and longing, and then I realized it is *her* grief at not having lived a *physical* life while she was in the physical world. When I returned to ordinary reality and my own life, I still carried the feeling of deep grief over the lost opportunity to enjoy an embodied, earthly life. While it came from an encounter with the spirit of someone long dead, the feeling had a poignant urgency that struck me deeply and personally.

This experience was pivotal in the healing of my ambivalence about being on this planet. I learned that the place we found Emily is called the Interworld, a kind of stasis for souls unable to transition to other levels of reality. The anguish I felt in Emily, stuck in that constricted space, full of remorse at not living a full physical life, stayed with me and began to resonate with my own way of living. The awareness of her experience after death, as I was shown it, drove me to want to avoid that same remorse. It was the beginning of my learning to embrace this life, emerging into a new way of being on earth.

In another journey soon thereafter, I encountered my ambivalence about being alive. My intention was to take a journey to experience my own physical death and to explore what happens after that death. My first feelings were ease, joy, and relief at detaching from my body and the physical world. I felt grief about leaving my children, but more strongly I felt drawn into the expansion and exploration possible in that new form. My senses felt wide open, and the potentiality felt vast, within a deep total silence. I yearned to stay there as long as I could, learning everything possible as I expanded more. Eventually, a voice tugged at me, saying, "It is not your time yet, you must come back, it is not time..." I came back because I must, but felt the tug toward that state of being, that "place" beyond this life on earth. After this journey, I better understand my way of living on this earth: carrying a strong yearning for that mystery beyond death, the yearning to escape (reminding me of how I first remembered the meaning of eschatology by the echo of that word "escape").

In another journey in this time, I again departed from the time of my own death and went far, far away to a place where spirits told me "humanity is not supposed to be." It was a place of total emptiness—with no presence or consciousness of human life—and I felt the possibility of getting totally lost and never coming back. Retaining the awareness of being an individual consciousness took great effort. I went toward a thick dense whiteness of light and then beyond that into further wide infinitude... I felt pulled further and further out, and in real danger of not returning. Finally, when the drum beat signaled the time to return, one part of me dragged the other part of me back, and it was not an easy task. The allure of the afterlife is a strong presence, palpable and powerful in these journeys.

One last journey to the time after my death gave me a deeper understanding of my personal resistance to this experience of life on earth. In this journey after dying, I was met immediately by my beloved grandparents who have both died. Nana and Papa surrounded me, and wrapped me in their arms, holding me as I repeated, "I cannot go on without this, I cannot go on without this..." For the duration of the journey, I was encircled by their love. When the drumbeat called me back to ordinary reality, I resisted coming back and lingered with them. I returned only when someone whispered in my ear that I *must* return now, as I had committed to doing. When I arrived back, I sobbed and sobbed about leaving that experience of infinite love and being back on earth without that.

These journeys exploring my own death, especially the last one, revealed critical truths about unconscious emotions and desires I was carrying. Soon after, as my marriage ended and family life changed, the awareness gained in these journeys became critical for my passage through those challenges and the others still to be revealed. This was the first unfolding of the shamanic death and rebirth process, although still only the prelude to the deepest part of the work. The necessary healing of what had been revealed unfolded in journeys yet to come.

SHAMANIC DEATH

In the fall of 2008, my helpers and teachers took me deeper into this excavation and dismemberment of my ego and sense of self. Shamanic death is a crisis, illness, or other challenge that breaks down and re-creates the self and thus one's relationship with Spirit. It is the crucible in which one is re-created, with a new way of being in the world, and in deeper connection with the spiritual realm. In the start of this phase, the breakup of my family was the challenge, although the challenges would become even greater as the descent continued.

Through this time, Tiger told me that although things may feel terrible, it does not mean they are bad. Isis said, "We are with you; we are tearing you apart. Just hold on, and we will bring you through it." In simple messages and in big journeys, Spirit was always present, and I had a tangible sense of being carried through whatever might happen. The sequence of journeys below maps my progression into and through this shamanic death.

I journeyed to ask for healing of grief about family breakup: A flock of birds carried me far, then dropped me on the ground. Snake appeared and said, "You are going to die," and began eating my body, part by part. Bear came to join in eating me, ripping my rib cage open, removing my heart and taking big bites out of it. Finally, I was devoured, all gone.

"You are nothing," I heard many times. I spent a long time

just hanging out in the nothingness, my body just a flat outline of what I had been, empty on the inside with blue light around the edges. Finally, Raven appeared in bird form, swallowed up the outline of my body, and again told me, "You are nothing now, you are empty." That message was repeated in later journeys: the presence of nothingness, the need to be in the emptiness. Raven said I am dissolving; I need to let go of more, so the emptiness will become even more true.

Another time, I journeyed to learn about letting go but I was also shown the necessity of conscious choice. To begin, I descended many levels, each time letting go of myself further, cutting cords that kept me tied to my body, and then even the cords that kept me tied to my spirit body. I became part of a swirling river, down to a deep quiet nothingness where I no longer existed. Then suddenly something reached down and pulled me up to an encompassing powerful light, the "all and everything." I was absorbed in the light, holding the everything, the fullness, and power of that light. Then I wondered, how will I find my way back home? "You don't have to leave," they said. "Of course I have to go back!" I responded. "No," they said, "You don't have to—you get to *choose*. You can stay or you can go back. You choose." After more back and forth like that, I finally understood: I could decide to stay on earth, or to leave my life if I so choose.

This decision to choose life was an ongoing process for a time, unfolding on the shamanic level. In my next journey, I was bound in something and couldn't move. My teacher Isis came, saying, "It's not done yet: this is your dead time, your winter. Hibernate…" I asked where this was headed, and I was shown a tunnel, all darkness inside with no light visible at the end. Lion and Tiger were on either side of me, bringing their protection, strength, and fierce drive to survive.

As this particular process unfolded, Bear became a more and more frequent presence. As the animal traditionally most associated with death and resurrection, he was the one who repeatedly devoured me, dismembered me, and took me to another place. Through September and October of 2008, Bear was present in every journey, and I was told over and over to let him carry me, and to "do nothing." "This time is all about stillness," I was told. Bear said I was learning to be held as he showed me being passed from one spirit to another, not ever alone. Spirit helpers told me again and again, "Be still, be held, and receive."

Bear told me, "Do nothing—you have no idea what is coming," and three days later I was diagnosed with breast cancer. The challenge to choose life moved to a deeper level.

In my first journey after that, I was told that this was a time of transformation in ways I could not understand at that point. Spirits said they will be "taking me for a while," as I needed to stay with them. I would "walk the earth again," but not yet. My coming back, they said, would depend on the love of people in my life, as those bonds would pull me back.

The next month was filled with doctor's appointments, the first surgery of that season, and questions on how to do all of this while my marriage was ending. The difficulty was overwhelming. In my next journey I asked, "What is called for now? What am I supposed to be doing?" This journey was the turning point, the moment when all that the spirits had shown me before became crystal clear, along with the imperative for me to change the direction of my soul's movement.

I journeyed to the lower world and was led through a tunnel to a big cavern. Ten to fifteen people were in a circle, seeming very somber or sad. They welcomed me and said we needed to decide things. They laid out crystals around us, and we smoked something. They told me we were deciding about my life, but I didn't really know what they meant. Raven came and lead me out of the circle, walking down a path. We were approaching a bright place; big light was filling the space. I suddenly realized what this might be, and stopped, saying, "Wait, I want to stay on earth!" "Are you sure?" Raven asked. Images of being alive—being in the ocean, sleeping outside, climbing a mountain, dancing, having sex—flooded my mind, and I insisted, "Yes, I want to be here." He told me, "It will be a fight" to stay—I would need to be absolutely determined, to lose all fear, and to trust the unfolding of life. "Whatever it may be," I repeated, "I want to stay on earth." So Raven turned me around, and we walked away from the light. He told me I wouldn't go there now. Back in the cavern, the people began to attach cords to my body and then pounded them into the ground. As they bound me to the ground, they told me they were reconnecting me to my life on earth. As I came out of the journey, my body felt heavier, like it had acquired more substance, was more weighted to the ground.

Just days after this journey, the oncologist gave me the treatment plan for the cancer: another surgery, then six months of chemotherapy. I began the process of grappling with medical realities, on top of the reality of our family breakup. The teachings from the journey echoed in me: my guidelines for getting through each day and moving toward health. I practiced being fierce about my decision and desire to survive, to stay embodied. Wendy brought me advice from her spirits, to "transition into the material plane as a beautiful vessel for the Divine, to feel the Divine in the bodily experience." I began a daily practice of meditation and contemplation, to focus on teachings from Spirit, and stay present with the challenges of current reality while affirming my commitment to life. With surrender and fierce determination, I was in constant dialogue with the spirits who were holding me through that time.

In another journey at this time, I was given an experience to help my healing. A vast being of blue light engulfed me, telling me that it was the spirit of Joy. Merged in this awareness of Joy, I heard, "Expand your consciousness…you are healed." I felt the big power of that spirit, as we (merged) saying, "I am Joy, I am

Joy." After the journey, I brought this into my days, focusing on the presence of Joy, and being held in a state of Grace. Part of my healing was learning to stay connected to the Divine through each challenge, knowing I am part of that mysterious Source of Being and Joy.

In this time of intense focus on healing, on both the medical and metaphysical levels, Raven stated that my body *would* heal from working directly with Spirit through the modes of work we were employing. While chemotherapy, Chinese herbs, and a healthy diet were necessary, spiritual growth and strengthening would ultimately create my healing. With this multi-faceted effort, I would eventually be totally fine, in every way.

However, the effort was not done. In multiple journeys, plus daily meditation, affirmations, and diving into Pema Chodron and other spiritual texts, I worked hard on the spiritual and psychological shift needed to survive. I was fighting to be alive on every level, and thus changing my way of being. Spirit remained close, like a teaching committee, a cheering squad, and a comforting presence when needed. My helpers and teachers were available anytime, for anything—comfort, inspiration, reminders of teachings, dietary advice, medical advice, rituals of release and clearing, or any other pieces of the healing process that were called for in a moment.

In this time, I wrote, *"Dance, pray, make love, meditate—that's what I want to do with my life. And then help others find their way, too. A spiritual counselor? Shamanic coach? Help with life path crises, questions, transformations..."* It was in this time of shamanic death and re-membering that the call to spiritual service appeared. I still had before me years of healing, study, and practice before I could begin that work, but the desire to share the gifts of this journey became clear to me at that point.

RE-MEMBERING: SHAMANISM IN SEMINARY

Months of chemotherapy ended, my husband moved out with the kids part-time, and my house was suddenly empty for days on end. Building up from the ground I knelt on, I began to recreate everything in my life. In contemplating going back to work, I felt that pull to bring Spirit into my work with people, and soon heard about a seminary that taught spiritual care from an "interfaith" approach. Seeing this as a way to do spiritual work with a wide range of people while retaining my own spiritual practice of shamanism, I enrolled at The Chaplaincy Institute in Berkeley in April 2010.

Thus began the phase of learning diverse traditions and spiritual care across a wide range of beliefs. Shamanism remained my spiritual foundation as I built upward, working with a bigger bag of tools, but it was a fallow time in some ways, a slow contemplation of how shamanism might fit into interfaith ministry. What part would it play?

Through the two years in seminary, bringing the shamanic approach to each faith tradition became the theme and the mode of my learning. Shamanism was the lens through which I came to understand the range of religions and belief systems. For the first time, I had direct communication with Baha'ullah, the spiritual teacher of my childhood religion. During a visit to a Hindu temple, I met the powerful presence of Vishnu, and that god became one of my spirit helpers for a short time. In the study and practice of Christianity, while saying the Lord's Prayer each morning, Jesus became a familiar presence, a spiritual being I could turn to for healing love. Without being a Baha'i, a Hindu, or a Christian, I could connect to these powerful spiritual beings as profound sources of teaching and healing. Bringing the shamanic approach to each faith tradition was my way to integrate and connect the multiple paths of spiritual belief and practice.

I also grappled with questions of cultural misappropriation and the politics of "Neo-shamanism." As a European white woman, do I have the right and the ancestry to claim shamanism as my primary practice? Core Shamanism is based on teachings and practices that are essentially universal, so I was not adopting any particular culture's traditions. Was this still misappropriation? With research, I learned that evidence of shamanic practice exists on every inhabited continent, and the most ancient paintings in the Cave of the Trois-Frères, in France, are understood to depict shamanic rituals. Learning that shamanic practices were world-wide, and underlie the emergence of all religions, allowed me to claim my own ancestral roots in these ancient practices.

Openly claiming my identity as an Interfaith Minister rooted in shamanic practice took a bit longer. Despite the extent of my experience with shamanism, and my strong connection with spirit beings in that realm, I was slow to bring this openly into my ministry. Coming from the culturally Christian background of the US, I grappled with the view that talking directly with spirits was something either dangerous or absurd. Whether it might be seen as delusion, as hubris, or as black magic, I feared it was incompatible with my role as Chaplain or Spiritual Director. I was hesitant to share my committed belief in the "reality" and the power of the spirit world, and my sustained relationship with beings in that realm.

RECOMMITMENT: INTEGRATION

Albeit slowly, I began to integrate this part of my identity, claiming it on both the spiritual and the professional level. As the nature of my particular ministry has evolved, the shamanic perspective has become part of all I do, whether explicitly or implicitly. Either as teacher, chaplain, or as spiritual director, I bring the understanding that Spirit manifests very differently for each of us. In whatever I do, I hold the awareness of the shamanic perspective and the presence of spirit helpers, and the readiness to share that experience when relevant or helpful.

Sometimes my sharing is with spiritual direction clients who already practice shamanism and want a director who is also practiced in that orientation. Other times it is interfaith seminarians who wish to understand this spiritual path and engage with it for a bit to learn the shamanic way more deeply. Sometimes I get to teach a room full of beginners this whole new way for them to connect directly with Spirit, bringing a shift in perspective on what is possible on the spiritual path. Or sometimes, someone in my world needs help listening more deeply to the call of Spirit, in a time of crisis or challenge, and I walk with them on the shamanic journey to find the light they are looking for.

The power of direct connection with Spirit is open to anyone through shamanic work, so I share this with others who are called to engage with Spirit in this way. The tools of shamanic practice are accessible and easy to learn. The practice is simple, but the path may be convoluted. Having a companion who has traveled the shamanic path can bring grounding and deeper integration to the process. My travels in this realm have given me tools to share with others, to support the exploration and healing they embark upon themselves.

The presence of a spiritual director or mentor can be the container for sustained pursuit of this path. Most of us need to be held and witnessed in our experience. When the shamanic work takes you into brambles and dark shadows, the presence of another person can be a golden thread of light connecting back to familiar and safe ground, a place to share and seek understanding of the shamanic experience.

Shamanism is a practice, and like any practice requires time, dedication, and patience. Transformation does not come in a weekend, and the sustained pursuit of healing and learning is accompanied by the continued presence of helping spirits. As it says in the Hadith Qudsi, when you take one step toward God/Allah, God/Allah takes ten steps toward you.

I once asked the spirits, "Why do you help us?" Isis told me, "To lighten the weight of human life so we spirits can soar." She is concerned with the uplifting of all souls, and humanity's experience affects that, for better or worse. Raven chimed in, telling me, "So I can feel the sun and wind on your wings." Meaning, as he said, that embodied human existence can be a wonderful thing, and since it is only here on earth that we expe rience that, it should be as good as possible. We are all connected, spirits, humans, and all living creatures, and they get to feel the good things we feel—it benefits them and all of us. Spirits help us because we help them, by contributing to humanity's movement forward, for the spiritual evolution of the whole.

At another time, I asked, "What do I have to learn on the Shamanic path?" I was shown a ring of people, hand-in-hand, circling around the whole world. This vision has remained strong in me, showing the ultimate purpose of shamanic work as well as all spiritual practice. May it be so.

4

MY SHAMANIC EXPERIENCES

JOHN R. MABRY

While I do not consider myself a practitioner of Core Shamanism, I have had several shamanic experiences, and have sought guidance from a few shamans. I have made shamanic journeys and have found many parallels to experiences common to the Christian tradition. In this section I will recount and reflect on some of these experiences.

EXCHANGE

A common practice in shamanism is the transfer of spiritual energies from one person to another. In a soul retrieval, the shaman may go in search of lost parts of a person who has sought her help. Once she finds the split-off parts, she "blows" them back into the person, restoring wholeness, health, and balance. This has echoes in other traditions, of course. In Buddhism, there is the practice of *tonglen*, the sending out of healing energy to another or into the world at large.

In the Christian tradition, this practice is known as "exchange." The archetypal example is Jesus, who felt his healing energy go out into the hemorrhaging woman in Mark 5:25-34.

Then, in his crucifixion and resurrection, he exchanged our sin for his grace. Such acts of exchange ripple out through time, being replicated in diverse ways. In the desert fathers, there is the story of Abba Lot:

A brother had committed a grievous sin. He went to Abba Lot, and was very nervous, unable to sit. Abba Lot said, "What is the matter, brother?"

He said, "I have committed a great fault and cannot acknowledge it to the priests."

The old man said, "Confess it to me, and I will carry it."

The brother said, "It's a bad one. I made sacrifices at the pagan temple and bought time with the sacred prostitutes there as well."

The old man rocked back and forth for a while. "This is not so bad," he said. "Don't be too hard on yourself. Go back to your cave, fast for a couple of days, and I will carry the blame for half of your transgression."[1]

Probably the most important exploration of exchange in Christianity is found in the writings of twentieth-century Anglican mystic Charles Williams, who placed the practice front and center in many of his novels and theological writings. Here is an example from his novel, *The Greater Trumps*:

Her hand closed round the ankle; her mind went inwards into the consciousness of the Power which contained them both; she loved it and adored it: with her own thought of Aaron in his immediate need, his fear, his pain, she adored. Her own ankle ached and throbbed in sympathy, not the sympathy of an easy proffer of mild regret, but that of a life habituated to such intercession. She interceded; she in him and he in her, they grew acquainted; the republican element of all created things welled up in them both. Their eyes exchanged news. She throbbed for an instant not with pain but with fear as his own fear passed through her being. It did but pass through; it was dispelled within her, dying away in the unnourishing atmosphere of her soul, and with the fear went the pain.[2]

Several years ago I had a dramatic experience of exchange myself. I had just been hired as editor of *Presence*, the international journal for spiritual directors. I was representing the journal at the annual conference for spiritual directors, which was being held close to home that year, in Burlingame. Unfortunately, when hired, I already had a prior commitment on my calendar to marry a couple that same weekend as the conference. Trying to honor all my commitments, I upset my boss by leaving my post at the conference Friday night to drive down to Santa Cruz for the wedding rehearsal. But as I left the conference center, a wave of fatigue washed over me that I feared would utterly overcome me. I had been working nonstop for days preparing for the conference, and the idea of driving down to Santa Cruz in Friday's rush hour traffic and back again seemed overwhelming. I was weary and literally staggering. I simply did not know how I was going to do it all.

Then, in a flash of irrational insight, I paused beside a large tree near the parking lot. I embraced the tree as far around as I could and begged it to help me. I told it how exhausted I was, and all that I had yet to do that day. And as I poured my heart out to this tree, I felt a mysterious energy pass from its bark into my skin. It was the oddest thing, and I'll never forget the feeling.

But whereas moments before I thought I might collapse, I was suddenly teeming with strange energy.

Riding on this renewed vigor, I hopped in my car and sped down to Santa Cruz. The wedding rehearsal went quickly, and before I knew it I was standing once again in front of the tree. I was speechless in my gratitude, and I simply said, "Thank you." I hugged the tree again, and I felt the strange energy leave me and enter back into the tree. But it didn't leave me as tired as I had been before. I still felt strangely renewed, though no longer buzzing with life as I had been.

Animism—the idea that everything in nature has a spirit—is another important aspect of shamanism. All things work together for the health and wholeness of the world. I had just experienced the compassionate spirit of this tree, who gave of itself to help restore me to balance. I wished there was more I could do than simply say, "Thanks." I wished there was a way to return the favor.

There was, but not to the tree. Ever since, I have been offering exchange in my spiritual direction practice. For instance, if I have a client who is suffering from extreme anxiety, I will offer to hold half of their anxiety. Do I literally feel it passing into my body? If they can let it go, yes. Is it uncomfortable for me? Not nearly so much as it is for them, since the anxiety is not mine. But it does offer them some relief, and it is a grace I am happy to pass on.[3]

VISIONARY EXPERIENCES

While I was in college, I was struggling mightily with the fundamentalist teachings I had grown up with and was terrified that God would reject me. At the time I was reading a lot of Anglican poets, theologians, and mystics. So on the day when a friend of mine said, "Let's go see what those Anglicans mean by 'church,'" I was primed for the experience.

Primed, maybe, but not ready. What I experienced that day when my friend Mike and I entered St. Michael's Episcopal Church changed me forever. First of all, I was blown away by the artwork. The Church of my childhood harbored a deep distrust of art or beauty, especially when it comes to adorning worship spaces. My jaw dropped when I encountered the gothic sanctuary, covered with tapestries, icons, and statuary. I was especially struck by the enormous, gory crucifix staring down at me in all its agony. I was mesmerized by it all and deeply moved.

But what really shook me was when the priest gave the call for communion. Although I cannot say why, I knew in that moment that I had found what I had been searching for all of my life. I raced for the communion rail and knelt.

And that's when it happened. I heard the voice of the Holy Spirit speaking to me. As the priest placed that wafer on my tongue, I felt a presence wash over me like an ocean wave, and I heard an audible voice, saying, "This is my mercy for you. You can feel it. You can taste it. It is real."

Today I see this as an Awakening experience, as Evelyn Underhill describes it in her book *Mysticism*. In an Awakening experience, a person is given a glimpse of unitive consciousness —usually unasked for and out of the blue. Most people are relieved when the experience passes, and go back to business as usual. But for some people, the experience changes the trajectory of their lives. I was one of those.

I have had many such experiences since, but probably one of the most dramatic happened just a couple of years ago. I was driving home from church, thinking about God's promise of renewal, when I had a mystical experience, an experience of breakthrough which was both ecstatic and terrifying at the same time.

In the flash of what must have only been a couple of

moments, I saw the Restoration of All Things—I saw all that was broken made whole, I saw people with their dignity restored, I saw an unbroken communion between humans and God, I saw peace between nations and love between neighbors. I saw the earth restored to beauty and balance. I saw all things in heaven and earth in harmony. It felt like an explosion in my brain, and in moments it passed, and I was left sobbing in my car, crying out over and over again to God, "Yes, yes, please, yes."

The experience is still vivid for me, and I am moved whenever I think of it. On the surface, it seems like an impossible hope. And yet, it is the very hope to which all of scripture, to which the teaching of Jesus, to which the assembled wisdom of our tradition points: the day is coming when God will restore all things, when everything that is broken will be healed, when all that has been lost will be found.

SHAMANIC JOURNEYS

Several years ago I had been wrestling with a lot of pretty heavy issues—issues of sexuality, identity, and the proper way ahead. I felt like I had exhausted every resource at my disposal for spiritual and personal discernment. Prayer seemed to be getting me nowhere, and I was finding no guidance within. I was almost desperate to discover some source of wisdom that might lend some insight to my situation. So when my therapist suggested I visit a shaman, I didn't bat an eye, I just asked for a phone number.

The shaman turned out to be a Jewish psychotherapist in Marin county who had been trained in Core Shamanism. In a preliminary shamanic journey, I was told I would be met by my power animal, who would be my guide in the other world. I was certain that my power animal would be a dog, since I have such an affinity for dogs. But the thing about power animals is that they pick you, not the other way around. So wouldn't you know it, I got a cat. A very *big* cat. A panther, in fact, came to me, announced himself, and stood rock still in one of the most awkward moments of greeting I can recall.

I am deathly allergic to cats. I'm sure there are some lovely cats in the world, but I have never been able to get close enough to one to get chummy. But *this* cat was not cuddly. In fact, Panther was just about the surliest fellow I have ever encountered.

On the day of my big shamanic journey, my shaman told me to get comfortable and instructed me to descend into a cave in my imagination. This I did. Panther met me in the cave and I explained my need for discernment that day. He listened dispassionately, as usual. Then he surprised me. As soon as I was done speaking, he pushed me down and lunged at my belly with his teeth.

I thought I knew the drill. I thought I knew what was going to happen. I did not expect to be attacked, especially with such force and violence. As I watched in horror, my guts spilled forth onto the floor of the cave. Panther hovered over me, and very deliberately stretched out his claws and began sorting. Turns out my belly was full of different colored yarn, all mixed up—a tangled mess, really. Panther was untangling the strands, grouping the threads of one color with those like them, and so on.

To my surprise, his big meaty paws were well suited to this work, and he displayed a nimbility that I would not have predicted. He pulled several strands of dark brown color out of me completely, coiled them into a hoop about the size of a coiled bullwhip, and set it aside. Then it was back to the sorting. Then, once again, he pulled something out of me. A much smaller black coil of threads. This, too, he set aside, and then returned to his task.

After several more minutes of this, Panther tied all the yarns of specific colors together—an amazing feat for a being with no opposable thumbs—and then gently placed the orderly mass back into my belly, sealing me up with a warm gust of breath.

As I got to my feet, I felt both renewed and shaky at the same time. "What are those?" I asked him, pointing at the two coils he had pulled out of me. He handed me the large, dark brown coil, and said, "This is your connection to your parents. Hang it on the wall, put it in a drawer, do what you want with it. It is no longer inside you, and it will no longer compel you."

I nodded with comprehension. They wouldn't be "pulling my strings" any more. My actions, thoughts, likes and dislikes would be my own. That alone, I knew—if true—would cut down on the anxiety and confusion I experienced much of the time.

"And the little one?" I asked him.

Panther handed me the small black coil. "This is your connection to god," he said. I took it and understood him to mean my connection to the god I had been given as a child, not the real God.

"What do I do with that?" I asked him.

"Give it back to God," he replied simply. By then I was hearing the drum signaling me to return to the surface, and as Panther turned to walk back into the recesses of the cave, I called after him, "Hey, why are you so surly?"

"Life is hard," he threw over his shoulder, and then he was gone.

I have had several experiences with shamanic journeys, but since it is not my tradition, it has never felt exactly right. It was a great relief when I discovered the practice of imaginal prayer as taught by St. Ignatius in his Spiritual Exercises. I have adapted this method for use in my daily prayer, and in leading others in prayer.

A couple of years ago, I was teaching a class at Santa Clara University in which I asked my students to get comfortable, to close their eyes, and to imagine that they were at work. I asked them to vividly imagine their work environment, their coworkers, the smell of the coffee in the break room, and so on. After giving them a few moments to orient themselves, I asked them to imagine that Jesus comes through the door. "Imagine that he comes straight up to you. He's striding confidently and smiling at you with a broad, open smile. He gives you a hug and asks you to introduce him to your friends and coworkers. Take fifteen minutes now to show Jesus around, introduce him to the other people in your office, and hear what he has to say."

Since there was so much time, and I wouldn't ask my students to embark on a journey I wasn't willing to take myself, I did the exercise too. I showed Jesus around another school I was teaching at, introducing him to the staff and my colleagues. Jesus was gregarious and appreciative, but once he'd met everyone he turned to me and said, "Let's get ice cream."

That was the last thing I was expecting, but who was I to argue? We walked to the nearby ice cream shop and got a couple of cones, then we sat on a low brick wall as we licked them. After a few seconds of awkward silence, Jesus got down to business.

"You know, John, you really need to let go of your ambition —it's making you miserable."

I froze. It was the last thing I'd expected him to say. I had been feeling like a bit of a failure at work at that time, especially in my pastoral role, because as hard as I tried, I couldn't seem to grow the small church I served beyond its twenty or so members.

"Are you talking about the church?" I asked.

He narrowed one eyebrow at me. "It's a form of greed," he said. "You should bloom where you're planted and be content with what you have."

I hadn't thought of it like that before. I thought it was my responsibility to grow the church, and the fact that I was not successful I took to be a personal failing. I had not seen it in terms of personal greed before. It was quite a wakeup call. I realized Jesus was gently and lovingly saying, "Knock it off," in terms of wanting a bigger congregation. He was being both compassionate and firm.

"Wow. Thank you," I managed.

He licked at his cone again. "This lust for fame of yours isn't going to serve you, or me, and you need to be careful of it in all of the areas you work in—books, music, teaching, pastoring. I mean, if you get it, watch out. It will distract you from your real work."

"What's my real work?" I asked.

"You're doing it," he said.

I felt a little rush of vertigo. The ice cream felt nourishing, comforting. It was a way to soften the blow. It was very sweet of him, and I found it moving. When I looked up at Jesus, I saw that he had a spot of ice cream on his nose. I also saw that he knew it, but he didn't wipe it off. I told him he looked goofy, and he didn't seem the slightest bit concerned. *What would it be like to be that secure?* I wondered. And I realized that I was being invited into just that kind of security.

I have taken that kind of prayer as a daily practice. If the sun is not yet up, I will find Jesus in his carpentry workshop. He is usually working on some kind of carving or furniture, and there is always a lovely fire blazing. He loves to tease me with a verse from the Gospel of Thomas—"Whoever is near me is near the fire." We sit in front of the fire, and he says, "Tell me what's in your heart." And I do. And sometimes he has some wisdom for me, but usually he just listens. Usually, he puts his arms around me and we cuddle a bit. It is very intimate, very nourishing, and very much prepares me emotionally and spiritually for my day.

"Now go and have a Friday," he says to me, if it's Friday.

"You'll be with me all day, won't you?" I ask.

"Every time you check in," he says, "you'll notice that I'm

there."

And that's true. That access is indispensable in my work as a pastor and spiritual director. I often joke that I don't actually do any pastoral work. I'm just a chauffeur. I drive Jesus from place to place, and he does all the work. I only present it as a joke because not everyone will understand it. In truth, I mean this quite literally. That is how I do my job. I just show up, going from place to place, bringing Jesus with me. He does all the heavy lifting. Every time.

This kind of imaginal prayer has become a cornerstone of my group spiritual direction work, as well, as at every session I invite people into an immediate experience of Jesus in imaginal prayer. Afterwords, I invite people to share and unpack the experience in the group. Sometimes what emerges is too intimate or scary to share with the group, but usually people are willing to share at least some of what they saw and heard. And their journeys with Jesus benefit all of us in the room.

This is not an exhaustive list of my visionary and shamanic experiences, but it will serve as a representative introduction. I have come to see such experiences not as unusual, not as aberrations, but as a daily, expected part of my spiritual life, and the spiritual lives of those I am privileged to serve. They are the norm, not the exception. The reason people do not hear more about them, I think, is that people (clergy included) are afraid to talk about them, scared that people might think them crazy if they did. This is a grave tragedy, because when people have visionary or mystical experiences—which happens frequently—they think they're sick or crazy. They are normal and healthy, but if no one tells them that, then how will they know? I am thinking that Mysticism Ed classes should be mandatory in all spiritual communities, just as Sex Ed classes are now common. Who's with me?

5

HEALING, KNOWLEDGE & GUIDANCE

DANIEL L. PRECHTEL

Come Holy Spirit,
we need your loving power.
With wisdom and your healing grace
visit us this hour.

Come our friend Jesus,
work in and through us.
Your world needs your presence,
peace, and restoration.

Come great Creator,
we are all your children.
Give us your blessing and
guide us in our living.

Come to us holy One,
true source and destination.
Be our companion, guardian,
and empowerer.

Great cloud of witnesses,
spirit friends come lend your aid.
Together let us do
our joyful work![1]

a t the time of this writing I have been an ordained Christian priest serving through the Episcopal Church for over thirty-five years and have served for nearly as many years as a spiritual director and guide. Since 2015 I have researched, learned, and practiced Core Shamanism. I realize that I have much ahead of me to explore and learn as a shamanic practitioner. And yet, there is much that I *have* learned and experienced in the field of Core Shamanism. In truth, for all the years I have practiced Christian forms of prayer and meditation, I approach these spiritual practices, along with my shamanic practices, with a "beginner's mind." Both core shamanic and Christian spiritual practices bring me into relationship with the great and ancient Mystery that desires to be with us, and to act with power and healing through us, for our benefit and the benefit of others.

I have known for many years that I am a "liminal" person—someone who stands at the threshold or boundary of realities. As such, I am keenly interested in exploring the parameters of consciousness and our perceptions of reality. Critical to doing that work is listening with the "ear of your heart"[2] and seeing with the eye of your heart.

As I was completing the first draft of my book *Light on the Path*, which concentrated on spiritual discernment practices, I came to realize that some of the elements of shamanism were a regular part of my ministry as a spiritual guide and in my own spiritual practice. Furthermore there are elements of shamanism in the priest's leadership in the sacramental rituals that bring the community into relationship with the power and grace of God through Christ Jesus and the Holy Spirit.

And yet there is a strong barrier that Western Christianity long ago constructed which makes exploring the worlds of nonordinary reality and developing relationships with helping spirits something that is often viewed with suspicion and considered fringe spirituality, even dangerous and psychotic, and out of bounds for reasonable people. That message was driven home to me early in my studies as a seminarian.

SEMINARY AND RATIONALIST CULTURE

In my first year as a seminary student I had a class in philosophical theology. Each of us was required to lead a discussion of an assigned reading topic. When my turn came I was to lead the class in considering Mircea Eliade's writing on "primitive consciousness." I came to class with a walking staff and began telling a story of when I once was in a section of my favorite woods and heard a grove of trees engaged in a conversation. I had chosen this story to tell because I had many experiences of merging my spirit with a tree and intuitively listening for what wisdom the tree chose to give or show me. It felt like a great privilege to then be allowed to "hear" trees in conversation. However, as soon as I mentioned this situation the professor commented, "And this is when I get nervous!"

Eliade was interested in the study of "primitive" worldviews, religions, and shamanism. Yet his Western rationalist cultural bias of superiority was evident in his language. My professor's worldview reflected Eliade's assumed superiority of Western modern thought and culture over the "primitive" consciousness of traditional cultures and I had clearly crossed his line of what was acceptable to consider in seminary. In the Western world we are too often taught a flat and shallow materialism that views nature as something we are set apart from and nature's myriad life forms as things to dominate and control. That is in stark contrast to a consciousness (which is far from "primitive") that respects everything in creation as having spirits linked together in a sacred web with the Holy One (called by many names) as the source and lover of all. As a consequence, our Western religious thinking always runs the danger of rigidly separating off the "sacred" from the "profane," the "spiritual" from the "material," and the "orthodox" from the "heretical."

SPIRITUAL EXPLORATION

Well before my seminary training my own spiritual yearning led me to explore ways in which I could build a direct relationship with the divine. Carlos Castaneda's books on the teachings of the Yaqui sorcerer and "man of knowledge" Don Juan Matus caught my attention and I practiced what I was able following the lead of these books without a guide. Over time I became convinced of the power of spirit beings and the existence of nonordinary reality. But ultimately my practice focused excessively on accumulating personal power and the directed use of my will for my own personal desires. It was a self-centered quest for power and I was tempted to view others as potential objects of manipulation. The result was an increasing feeling that I was losing the best values of my humanity and spiraling into an emotional, spiritual, and mental darkness that was frightening. In my late twenties a vivid and terrifying dream warned me to forsake this path and return to my spiritual roots and relationship with Jesus Christ.

When I heeded the dream and went back to the Christian faith I joined an Episcopal church. I discovered that there was much I could learn about the many possible varieties of prayer and meditation. Membership in a small charismatic group of Roman Catholics and Episcopalians was a starting place for some of my exploration. It was in that small group that I experienced the effects of the imminence of the Holy Spirit, working directly within and among us, bringing spiritual gifts to bear on our needs and concerns for others. Prayer in that group was spontaneous, intuitive, and deeply compassionate. Some of our members spoke in tongues or interpreted what was spoken. Others exercised other gifts of the Spirit, such as wisdom or knowledge or prophecy. Prayers for healing, with the group laying their hands on the member requesting God's healing grace, were occasionally offered.

CHRISTIAN SPIRITUAL HEALING

The charismatic group was not a formal part of my church community's offerings to parishioners. Charismatic groups within mainline churches have often been viewed by the church leadership as a divisive and threatening force—sometimes with good reason and other times out of fear of losing control. However, in my church we had a healing prayer group that gathered regularly. Some members were regular attenders and some only came as they felt the need for receiving healing prayer. In that group, as in the charismatic prayer group, the person requesting healing would be surrounded by the others. We would lay our hands on the person's head and shoulders and offer spontaneous prayers for Christ's healing.

The Episcopal church that I attended also offered a sacramental healing rite as part of the Friday noon Holy Eucharist. Those wanting healing were invited to come to the priest, who would anoint the forehead of the petitioner with blessed oil, lay hands on their head, and pray for God's grace for the person's healing needs.

Friday noon service became a very important resource for my own healing needs as a young man. I worked near the church and could often take my lunch hour attending the service. When I went through a year-long period of grief and depression due to the breakdown of my marriage and eventual divorce I found deep consolation in receiving sacramental healing alongside Holy Eucharist on a regular basis. The Holy Eucharist reminded me that I was objectively connected with others and with God's love in sharing communion even if I usually felt desolated. The sacramental rite of Unction of the Sick was available for anyone seeking God's grace for the healing of their body, mind, or spirit, and I experienced the comfort of the assurance of God's healing grace in that dark time. Both of these sacramental rites provided a path toward a new wholeness through the immediate presence of God's love and power in the midst of my experience of brokenness.

That Friday noon service also served prominently on the occasion of one of my children's health problems. She had chronic throat infections and was a candidate for having her tonsils and adenoids removed. But in preparation for surgery her blood platelet testing showed an abnormally slow clotting time, which would increase her surgical risk. The blood testing was repeated a number of times and it continued to show the same results. Her physician and the surgeon consulted others but were unable to understand what was causing the slow platelet clotting factor. Finally I brought her to the Friday noon healing service and asking healing for the slow blood clotting. After that her blood platelet testing showed a normal clotting time and she was able to have the surgery.

However, following the surgery her voice sounded constricted for a period of time past normal healing and it began to concern her surgeon in follow-up visits. So I took her to another service for the healing rite and her voice then became normal. Whatever the reason—physiological or due to a defensively constrained use of her vocal chords—she received a spiritual healing manifesting in the cure of that condition.

SPIRITUAL HEALING IN MY PARISH MINISTRY

When I was ordained in 1984 and began serving a parish church in Michigan, one of my initial goals was to introduce the congregation to the regular availability of the Church's sacramental healing rite. This was new to the congregation and most of the parishioners were fairly conservative in most ways, including what was offered at Sunday worship.

Although the 1979 *Book of Common Prayer* had been out for five years, it was apparent that they had not engaged much of what this revision of the prayer book offered. Many incorrectly associated the healing rite with the Roman Catholic last rites offered on the death bed. I had to teach them that this is not only available to those who are hospitalized—and not just for those *in extremis*—but available to anyone seeking God's grace for the healing of spirit, mind, and body. This sacramental rite of healing could be offered at a church's normal public services, like on Sunday worship. There was also skepticism about the efficacy of spiritual healing rites since most people's major point of reference was what they saw as faith healing exhibited by television evangelists.

I was able to lead them into having a monthly Sunday service that included the sacramental healing rite available to anyone who desired it following the Holy Eucharist. Gradually, some people responded. After some time I trained several parishioners to assist me in offering the healing rite and we later made it available at a regular midweek Holy Eucharist service. Later, on the Sunday closest to the October 18 feast day commemorating St. Luke the Evangelist (the "Beloved Physician"), we offered a public service of healing at the main Eucharist, and some parishioners brought friends to this special service focused on the church's healing ministry.

The efforts to bring God's spiritual power to heal people as an extension of Jesus' own earthly healing ministry was not new, but it had been mostly restricted to the arena of charismatic circles or evangelistic rallies and conferences. To quietly and gently make sacramental healing opportunities a normal part of a parish church's ministry and worship was still a new thing in the mid-1980s. Mainline Christian churches had relinquished their part in healing people in favor of a Western medical approach that had no real part for the Spirit to do direct healing work. Now a spiritual healing ministry was emerging that could be understood as complementary to the dominant culture's accepted medical practices. The emerging spiritual healing practices were not intended as a replacement for Western medical practices, but to intentionally bring God's spiritual grace and power to the one requesting healing.

STORIES OF HEALING IN THE PARISH

It is hard to assess how spiritual healing impacts most people who come seeking it because we do not usually follow up with people about their experience of public healing rites. We simply offer the healing rite, asking God's healing grace for the person seeking it, and trust that the person does receive help. People come for various reasons. Sometimes they ask for emotional healing, sometimes it is for the healing of relationships, or seeking relief from a physical ailment, or in anticipation of surgery, in times of grief and loss, or in seeking work or some other social need. We say that it is available for anyone seeking God's healing grace for body, mind, or spirit. When I offer laying on of hands and anointing with oil for healing, I ask the spirit of Jesus to merge with me and let my hands also be the healing hands of Christ. I ask the Spirit to guide and empower the healing that the recipient needs.

The healing that is received can be of several types: healing matters of the spirit, spiritual healing with a physical cure, and spiritual healing without a cure.[3] I wish to share a few stories from my pastoral experience that illustrate these dimensions of healing.

One time I went with parishioners who were ready to be confirmed, received, or wished to reaffirm their baptism to a "round-up confirmation service" with a bishop at our cathedral. As we gathered at the cathedral, one of my parishioners arrived with a patch over an eye. We asked her what happened and she said that she had accidentally burned her eye with a hot curling iron and had just left the emergency room. She reported that the burn was bad and she was expected to return to have her eye examined again the next day. When the time came she went forward and the bishop laid his hands on her head and prayed for the Holy Spirit's grace and empowerment of her. She remarked afterward that she definitely felt something powerful happen to her. The next day she met with the physician to have her eye examined and was told that there was no sign of any injury. The doctor couldn't explain what had happened because the burn had been so serious. My parishioner attributed it to the healing power she received at the previous day's confirmation prayer.

Another parishioner who suffered from Crohn's disease for many years was recovering from recent colon surgery and some of us gathered with her at her home. We celebrated a simple Holy Eucharist and then laid hands on her and anointed her, asking for God's healing grace and power. She maintained for the years I knew her afterward that she was cured from Crohn's disease on the occasion of that gathering.

A third story is more complex. "Martha" was a senior who, along with her husband, was very active in the parish. She came down with a form of life-threatening cancer that put her into hospice care. At one point she was hospitalized for palliative surgery and in the course of a pastoral visit we offered healing prayer for her. The palliative surgery was on a nerve and she was then pain free. She returned home and resumed her activities, including church, and occasionally received healing prayer, and after a few months she reported that the cancer was in remission and she was no longer under hospice care. She was a hospice dropout!

A little while later Martha and her husband attended a "Circle of the Spirit" group I ran at church. This was a small group designed to introduce a variety of spiritual practices and exercises to give parishioners a broader set of spiritual resources to draw on in support of their relationship with the Divine. At one session I led the group in a depth guided meditation I had crafted, drawn from Revelation 3:20. Those in meditation envisioned Jesus knocking at the door of their home. The meditators let Jesus into their home and they were invited to engage with him in any way that felt right. When the meditation was over I asked if there was anything that people wished to share about what occurred. Martha, radiant with wonder and joy, said that she never knew that Jesus loved her so much! The love she was given by him was surprising, overwhelming, and beautiful. She also felt that she needed to pass on some of the love she experienced and wished to change the way she acted with some of her family. For about a year she initiated and worked through mending relationships with some close family members where she had been overly critical.

After about a year, on the Sunday closest to St. Luke's feast day, we held a special service of public healing along with our Holy Eucharist. Martha was one of the people who came forward for the rite of healing. Later that day I received a phone call from Martha's husband. He calmly reported that Martha had just died. I came over to their house immediately. I said I was so sorry and I was baffled by the timing of her death. It was just a few hours ago that she received healing prayer. Her husband gently said that Martha had peacefully died while quietly sitting on a recliner chair watching television. What could be an easier way to die than that? From his perspective this was a graceful spiritual healing for God to now receive her in such a gentle way.

Family members who had been in tension with Martha for a long time mentioned how much she had changed in the past year and were very grateful for the reconciliation and love they had experienced with her. Martha was given the gift of having additional time to do her inner work and complete important unfinished business with family members. The spiritual healing and love she received from Jesus Christ had swept through her family system.

HEALING IN SPIRITUAL DIRECTION

Sometimes in my spiritual direction practice I pray with a client about a healing need. The prayer can take many forms, including meditations. I have worked with clients in healing the spiritual and emotional damage they received in the past. We have done inner child healing work together. On some occasions a client has suffered from a strained or broken relationship and found healing in envisioning a three-way conversation with the other and Christ or the Holy Spirit advocating peace, healing, and transformation. With one client who suffered major depressive episodes over many years we worked to bring the negative or abusive inner persons into the steady and healing presence of Christ. What began as internal personas that accused and blamed and bullied her became an "inner committee" of wisdom and strength and support due to the transforming mediation of Christ's firm and consistent love and care for both the internal personas and for the suffering person.

INNER SACRED VILLAGE

Over time I developed several meditations where there are "inner" or "spiritual" locations for engaging helping, tutelary, or ancestral spirits. These became two of a larger group of places in what has become my "inner" Sacred Village. All the structures of the Sacred Village are protected from intrusion by Middle World spirits as consecrated ground. If a spirit enters the space it is only by my invitation. These various inner places are particular to my own spiritual life, but you may envision similar constructions.

Wisdom's House. The first place that I envisioned was a meeting place with Wisdom. This was born out of my desire to seek God's spirit of wisdom and guidance in the decisions and life situations that come my way. The meditation is essentially a prayerful tool for requesting divine guidance and help in matters of discernment. I was struck by the poetic vision of Wisdom's generous hospitality in Proverbs:

> *Wisdom has built her house,*
> *she has hewn her seven pillars,*
> *She has slaughtered her animals,*
> *she has mixed her wine,*
> *she has also set her table.*
> *She has sent out her servant girls,*
> *she calls from the highest places in town,*
> *"You that are simple, turn in here!"*
> *To those without sense she says,*
> *"Come, eat of my bread*
> *and drink of the wine I have mixed.*
> *Lay aside immaturity, and live*
> *and walk in the way of insight."*
> *—Proverbs 9:1-6*

The meditation I use to journey to Wisdom's House (sometimes I have called it the house of the "Inner Wise One") or to guide someone else in meditation to get there is quite simple.[4] I visualize a footpath that runs through a meadow and then up a hill. Wisdom's house is on the left side at the top of the hill. I go to the door of the house and knock. I enter when Wisdom opens the door or calls to invite me in. I look around the room and notice how Wisdom appears to me, which varies from visit to visit. I discuss my concern with Wisdom and am attentive to whatever this Spirit gives me in reply. I may be shown something, or told something to guide me.

A Journey for Discernment at Wisdom's House. When I first began studying and exploring the core practices and cosmology of shamanism at the beginning of 2015, I was very concerned that I would be able to do this with integrity and be faithful as a Christian priest and follower of Jesus Christ. I went to my spiritual director and asked him to lead me in this meditation to visit Wisdom with the question of whether this exploration of shamanism is part of my vocational calling.

I started the journey on a dirt path. I could feel the earth beneath my feet. On my right side was a forest, and on the left was a meadow. The path slowly ascended a hill. Before I began to walk I was joined (unplanned) by Bear from the woods and Lion from the meadow. They posted themselves on either side of me and accompanied me in my meditation. I was happy to see them. They are symbols/archetypes that have come into a number of my dreams and some meditations. I began to walk uphill and when I neared the top I saw a small house, tidy but very simple and modest. I had an association with a dwelling of a desert mother or father. There was a planter on the side of the house that had flowers in it. I walked up two steps in the front of the house to the door and knocked. Bear and Lion waited outside. I was invited to come in.

Wisdom appeared as a human-like being, with a light glow around the head, and the face seemed to be constantly shifting between male and female features. I was welcomed and immediately given a cup of hot cocoa! I was delighted and surprised and thought that it was great for my inner child!

Wisdom asked me what I wished to consult her about, and I told her (she seemed more female then). When I asked Wisdom what I should do, the first response was a great big beaming grin. I was surprised and a bit relieved by her grin and began to weep. She said that I'd already been doing this kind of inner journey work personally and with people for many years. I should take it step by step. I asked Wisdom how I was to know what the right path was and that I was doing the right thing and her reply was for me to "follow the way of the cross." I took this to mean not being self-centered but acting with humility; being a faithful follower and representative of Jesus Christ, and participating in God's work of healing, reconciliation, liberation, and restoration of all things into God's unity.

I felt that I received Holy Wisdom's guidance and thanked her/him, saying that I would like to return again for other visits. S/he gave me a generous, warm, luminous embrace and I again began to weep at receiving such love. I felt so very deeply blessed. I went back outside and my companions, Bear and Lion, were waiting for me. I walked down the hill and then thanked my animal companions, telling them that I would like to see them again and get to know them better. I then returned to normal consciousness.

This was a turning point in my discernment around whether I can be faithful to my calling as a Christian priest, and yet also be a shamanic practitioner. I gained clarity about my purpose and conduct in doing the shamanic work as my way of following "the way of the cross" and Jesus.

Jesus at Wisdom's House. A few months later I did another "Wisdom's House" journey while I was alone in the chapel at my church. In this visit I recognized Jesus as the wisdom figure. He welcomed me and spoke quite matter-of-factly about how this is what I am to do, this is part of my mission in healing, understanding, and reconciliation. There seemed to be no problem with my desire to explore these realities. He told me that I could call upon his help any time if I felt I needed it. I told him that I would like to go on missions from him. He said that the time would come for me to do that but at the beginning he wanted me to just explore and get to know the helping spirits.

My Grandfather. I also had gotten into the practice of inviting Lion and Bear to be unseen (in ordinary reality) companions in my daily walks along the bay trail. On one of those walks Lion told me that my deceased grandfather, who was an ordained minister, understands and isn't disappointed in my shamanic journeying. I took that to heart. I would in no way want to disrespect this ancestor who has been very important to me.

Each of these was, in the language of shamanism, a "divination journey" and contributed to my discernment about engaging in shamanic practices. These consultations with helping spirits were part of a larger process that included discussions with my spouse, my spiritual director, some of my relatives, and other colleagues in the fields of spiritual direction and ordained ministry.

The Healer's House. Paralleling Wisdom's house is the house of the Healer in my Sacred Village. I envision the journey to get there as the same way from the meadow to the top of the hill, with the Healer's house located on the right side of the path. The Healer is a compassionate spirit of the Divine, like Wisdom. The meditation is similar to the visit to Wisdom.[5] In the visit I talk to the Healer about my healing needs and then receive what is offered. I might receive healing touch, or see a healing light permeate my body where there is an affliction, or receive guidance, or some other response from the Healer. I am free to converse and ask questions to help clarify what is occurring or needs to occur. Like with the meditation on visiting Wisdom, I have guided others as well as used it myself.

THE MANSION

This part of my village first came to me in a dream that I mentioned in *Light on the Path*. In that book I also offered a guided meditation on exploring the Mansion. We will all see the inner Mansion differently since it is reflecting and speaking to your particular truths and understanding. In my Sacred Village, the Mansion is located on the path beyond the hill and to the right.

I sometimes call this "my" Mansion but it is actually owned by the Host who appears at times to me as a large and radiant presence. When I first went to the Mansion (in a dream) I did not go beyond the large, majestically carved wooden doors into the foyer because there were two big strong dogs, Doberman Pinschers, that approached and silently stood guard. I didn't feel ready to see if they would let me enter. It took me nearly a year before I had enough clarity and sense of purpose to risk entering past the guardians. When I did take a step into the Mansion I was greeted by wagging tails and a little further down the foyer I was met in welcome by the Host, who appeared as a large gentle glowing Light.

Living Room. I have seen some of the rooms in the Mansion but there are others yet unexplored. The Living Room is a fascinating place. Here I have met people close to me, or those who have died who were close to someone on whose behalf I was journeying. I have talked to a dear grandfather there, several parishioners who have died, and made a visit on behalf of a bereaved mother for her infant child. I first got the idea of the Living Room from a meditation by Carolyn Stahl Bohler in *Opening to God: Guided Imagery Meditation on Scripture.* Bohler offers a meditation based on John 14:1-4 for visiting someone (living or dead) who has left you and to whom you wish to say goodbye. Many years ago I led a young woman using that meditation as she yearned to say some final words to her father who had died unexpectedly. The conversation she was able to have with her father in the room that God had prepared for him was very powerful and loving.

Ballroom. On one All Saints' Day I decided to make a journey to the Mansion to see if I could visit some of the saints. I went to the Living Room, but it was empty, and I told the Host about my desire to visit the saints. I wondered if there was enough space there and instantly I was transported to a huge Ballroom. There was a beautiful swirling host of saints all dancing together in a kind of line dance pattern that would spiral around the huge space—and I was part of this immeasurable gathering. At times I could discern particular beings: some of my spirit animals were there; and I saw Benedict and his sister Scholastica (whom I had just taught about in a class at church). Francis of Assisi was there, and we reminisced and laughed together about the time that he taught me a dance in the woods. I caught glimpses of some departed family members. I saw a bishop who had once served as my spiritual director. I saw Jesus and we briefly spoke to each other about a concern I had for someone. At times the pattern of movement became circular, with the center being opened to the Godhead, unseen but full of power and love. Curiously, I did not hear music as an external sound, but it seemed to vibrate deep within me and permeate the area soundlessly. On another All Saints' Day I returned to the Mansion's Ballroom out of curiosity and the music supporting the dancing saints was Irish and Scottish. It was all quite fun and a lively celebration.

THE MONASTERY

As a Benedictine oblate, I serve as a representative of Benedictine spirituality in the world at large and am in a vowed relationship in support of a particular monastic community, St. Gregory's Abbey in Three Rivers, Michigan. These men follow the Rule of St. Benedict that was written in the sixth century. In my nonordinary spiritual Middle World the abbey that I know provides the basic structure for the monastery that I envision. I get to the inner Monastery by continuing the path over the hill, and after a curve it is located on the left side of the path. There are some differences, of course, in the inner Monastery. Instead of being just for men, the inner Monastery is a dual community, which is to say that it is a monastic community for both men and women. The Monastery church is about the same as in ordinary reality. Below are some special features of the Monastery.

Library. The ordinary reality abbey has a very fine library, but the Monastery Library is vast and multilevel. I have the sense that it is connected to a universal library system and perhaps to the Akashic Records. I have yet to do much research there.

Elevator. There is an Elevator in the inner Monastery and it is operated by a particular monk, Brother Aloysius. This monk will take me to levels of either the Upper World or Lower World. I sometimes ask the brother to take me to a level where I can find someone or some place.

Visiting the Angels' Realm. For example, on the feast day of St. Michael and All Angels, I once asked the Elevator brother to take me to the Upper World where angels gather. He took me to the seventh level (of course! seventh heaven!) and let me out. I stepped into thick white cloud/fog that made it hard to see. (I was amused as I thought of the many popular pictures of angels on clouds.)

I called out for a guide to help me. An angelic being came to me right away, introduced himself as Gabriel, and greeted me by name. "Gabriel," I mused. "Archangel and principal communicator from God to humans. Fitting." Although I was astonished that such a powerful being would choose to be my guide. I couldn't see much of Gabriel in the thick cloudiness. He appeared like a large and strong man. He told me to put my wings on and follow his lead.

I did so, and we rose above the cloud and flew to where the clouds cleared away and I could see a large complex that had a castle-like appearance. Then we landed in a large square near an outdoor café. I put away my wings in my backpack and sat down opposite Gabriel. He ordered tea for us, which tasted like sweet nectar. All this time I "knew" where I was and could see vaguely, but I couldn't really visualize the angel with clarity. So I told him that I couldn't see him. He then appeared in a slightly enlarged human form but his head and face glowed with radiant white luminescence and the features were unrecognizable.

I asked Gabriel more about angels, and he told me that they usually appear as human-like—but that is a gloss. They are shapeshifters and normally appear in a way that people can receive them. That also seems to be the case with many other helping spirits. Angels also live outside time and space restrictions, as do many other Upper and Lower World beings. I had the clear impression that they want to help humans in their Middle World experience. I asked about guardian angels and Gabriel affirmed that we humans have them. I could consider my animal spirit helpers in that way, but I wasn't given or introduced to a particular angel that was defined as my guardian angel. That was something for me to explore another time. Gabriel affirmed that there were "fallen angels" that are part of the Middle World struggle. I asked if there is any hope for their eventual reunion with the angels that serve the Divine. He considered that a possibility but it didn't seem certain.

I told Gabriel about my impressions in journey visits with Jesus. Jesus seems unpretentious and almost ordinary, yet deeply knowing and fully present. He doesn't come across as the most powerful being/God of all that is. In our Christian language we emphasize Jesus' lordship and sovereignty. He doesn't come across that way or fill me with fear and awed reverence. I believe he is all of that. But the feelings I have of him on these journeys are of friendship and complete trust. I know I am loved and I feel love in return. I want to follow him, for he is the source of wisdom for me. Gabriel said that Jesus uses his power to build good and healthy relationships and shares it generously for the well-being of all. Jesus does not wield power from the top down as an autocrat would.

Time was nearing the end for my journey. Gabriel asked me if I would like to see the Heavenly Council. I said yes. He told me to put my hand on his shoulder and I was instantaneously in another location. I saw a huge gathering of beings. It seemed rather like a United Nations gathering, with seating for the many, many angelic beings. They were in concentric circles radiating out from a grand center that was a living Being of Light that appeared like an immense spherical Presence. The image I got was like seeing our galaxy from a great distance, with a large dense central spherical cluster of stars, and then radiating out from the center the immense breadth of other stars on a flatter plane—but the stars were angelic beings. There was a dynamic flow of movement where some angels would arrive at the Council and some would leave on missions.

Apothecary and Infirmary. Another feature of my inner Monastery is its Apothecary and Infirmary. At times I have received healing help for myself and others from these spiritual resources. The pharmacist, Br. Irenaeus, has given me small, expandable "healing globes" that are concentrated balls of healing light that I have shared with several people on occasions of need. I was a patient in the Infirmary when I had severe hemorrhaging in my lower GI tract.

The Meeting Place. All of the aforementioned structures were part of my meditation practices before I began making formal shamanic journeys, although they were further developed once I was engaged in shamanic practices. What began as a product of early shamanic journeying was envisioning the Meeting

Place. The structure of this area is very simple and is drawn from a regional bay trail that I walk in ordinary reality virtually every day. It is at the conjunction of meadow, woods, and an ocean bay, with mountains in the background.

There is a coastal redwood tree that is near the shoreline of the bay. Facing the redwood tree and the bay is a simple wooden bench. When I first started making shamanic journeys, I visualized a coastal redwood tree or a giant sequoia (forms of the World Tree) to travel to the Upper and Lower World, entering a hollow in the tree's center and then traveling up or down. The wooden bench is often where I meet Jesus.

The Meeting Place is, like the other structures in the Sacred Village, a place set apart for meeting my compassionate helping spirits and teachers that come from the Upper and Lower Worlds. The Meeting Place has been very useful in calling together my spirit helpers and teachers when I want to get their advice and counsel on a question or concern in my life or on behalf of someone who wants me to consult my spirits. Or I may gather a team of helping spirits (such as gathering a power animal spirit, and an angel, with Jesus as overseer) at the Meeting Place in preparation for a particular mission of healing.

The inner sacred village is the usual way I am able to envision a location or a departure point for healing and divination journeys, but one doesn't need to create a village in order to engage in shamanic journeying. Basically the practitioner "sees" a structure (such as a tree or hole in the ground) that is a platform for travel to the Upper and Lower Worlds and for meeting their helping spirit(s).

FURTHER STORIES OF HEALING AND DIVINATION

In Chapter 2 I described the kinds of shamanic healing and divination that I am most familiar with and have personal experience in practicing and receiving. I have left out descriptions of the kinds of practices that are outside my experience, such as shamanic journeys for plant medicines and how to use them, or describing a wide variety of Middle World spirits. The following are additional examples of my experiences of practices referred to in the earlier chapter.

Guardian Spirit Retrieval. I have made journeys to the Upper and Lower Worlds to seek out potential helping spirits for myself, or to visit a helping spirit I work with in its normal setting, but I also make journeys on behalf of others to find a guardian spirit. As previously discussed, from the shamanic perspective it is important to have a helping spirit to assist us in staying healthy, and to give counsel and empowerment in our living. Often guardian spirits appear as power animals in traditional shamanic visions. Those who live without a helping spirit are undefended and subject to power losses and illness and so it is important, from a shamanic perspective, for people to have a working relationship with such a helping spirit.

When I make a journey to retrieve a guardian spirit for a client, I travel to the Lower World and call out that my client needs a spirit helper and I ask for a power animal that is willing to work with my client. I then begin walking and looking for the spirit. There may be several kinds of animals that appear in my journey. I look for multiple appearances of a power animal in the journey as a confirmation that this spirit offers itself to the client.

For example, in one instance of retrieving a power animal, I first saw a beautiful stag deer that was near a bush. Then I saw several different birds as I continued my walking journey. Later I saw a doe and a buck together near a stream. Finally, I saw the stag again in a meadow. Since that was the fourth deer I saw, I came up to the stag and asked it if it was willing to be a helping spirit for my client. It indicated it was willing. So I then gathered the spirit in my hands and returned to the Middle World. My client was lying next to me and I blew the spirit into his chest/heart region and the top at the back of his head. Then I used a rattle to seal the helping spirit's presence with my client. I told the client which power animal was now with him and he agreed to work with the deer as a helping spirit.

Spirit Intrusion Extractions. Sometimes low-level spirits are able to penetrate our life force field when we are vulnerable and lodge in us. We may experience localized pain or discomfort or other problems in the region where the intrusive spirit has penetrated. Discomfort or persistent illness is the usual complaint when a client seeks the help of a shamanic healer, sometimes alongside the services of a medical practitioner.

As previously mentioned, these can be "thought forms" that are hurled at us in anger or intentionally cast as spells. More frequently they can be spirits we happen to pick up like bloodsuckers lurking in water, or cling-tight weed seeds, or ticks waiting in a field for a host. They aren't necessarily evil or malevolent but they don't belong attached to a human being. The shamanic practitioner envisions or otherwise senses the intrusive spirit while merged with a helping spirit, and has a process for removing it from the afflicted person. Intrusive spirit extraction is a very common shamanic healing practice for the spiritual dimension of illness. It is very common for people to pick up spirit intrusions, and so clearing them is a very underused healing resource in this culture.

When I work with a client to extract intrusive spirits, I frequently merge with one particular power animal who specializes in this work. Often I experience the merged state with this animal in doing this healing work as joyous, powerful, and compassionate—but also very matter-of-fact and dedicated to getting the job done efficiently. I have no doubt that this power animal is directly linked to God's divine healing power (as are all of my helping spirits).

When I am merged with my power animal for extraction work I see the intrusive spirits as nasty little coiled snakes, or living things that look like barbed wire, or cutworms, or insects with pincers, or black and nasty blobs. They always appear to me in such a way that I can recognize them as unwanted spirits that cause harm. Unless specifically asked, I don't describe the spirit that I see because the form it takes is for my own sight and not that of the client. After the extractions and cleaning I normally just tell the client that whatever doesn't belong has been removed.

With one client I saw little coiled snakes both on the right side of her neck and in her lower spine and something like electricity running between those sites. However, the client hadn't mentioned any particular locations of pain before I began the extraction work. After the removal of those intrusive spirits the client told me that she had been bothered by neck pain and the treatment was "spot on."

Another client had generalized complaints of fatigue and depression before I began the extraction work. In my merged state I saw and removed major infestations of intrusive spirits in two sites in her body. But then I saw a third site on one knee and removed those intrusions. After the removals the client remarked that she forgot to tell me that she had recently hurt that knee and it had given her pain!

Power animals are not the only spirit allies that can help with spirit intrusions. In some situations I ask St. Raphael, an archangel known as the bringer of God's healing power, to be with me and help in healing work. One of my spirit teachers has also provided healing in various ways.

A case in point is a surprising incident of healing I received from a spirit teacher that appears to me as a Native American. It was early in my relationship with this spirit teacher, and I visited him at his modest hut in a small village in the first level of the Upper World. He invited me into his hut, I opened the leather flap that served as a door and went in. We sat together on some furs on the dirt floor near the central fire. I asked him if there was something he wanted to teach me or show me. His face then became the face of an eagle and he began pecking at my brain with his fearsome curved beak. He removed and spit out gouts of black stuff that was lodged in different parts of my head. When he finished and his face returned to his normal appearance I asked him what he had done. He told me that he had removed "plantings of ignorance and false assumptions."

I thought about the racism and sexism and other cancerous things that had been planted in my mind since my childhood. I thought of the narrow, fear-based, and militant views of a diminished Christianity that hamper my understanding and my experience of God's generous grace and love. I want to be cleansed of such things—these sick, spiritually-transmitted "thought forms" that are cultural impediments to knowing a greater reality and the right ways of being in relationship.

Soul Retrieval. This healing practice is designed to restore split-off parts of the client's soul after traumatic events or sometimes chronic illnesses. One of my clients expressed a desire to feel more confidence in herself and sought help. After a divination consultation suggested soul retrieval, I and a team of my helping spirits journeyed to find and retrieve a portion of her lost soul that was displaced. Her "lost" soul portion appeared in a dark interworld location. The soul portion looked like the client. I told the separated soul portion that the client needed her to come back and asked if she would be willing to journey with me to unite with her. After consent was given, the lost soul joined me and my healing team and came back to the client. I united the lost portion to the client in a way similar to guardian spirit retrievals.

Sometimes the soul of a body part becomes split off from the rest of the body due to trauma. In one situation the client felt a little out-of-sorts but wasn't aware of any particular need. I did a divination journey and one of my helping spirits suggested I perform a soul retrieval. This was the case when a client wasn't clear about any particular need but in a consultative journey one of my helping spirits suggested I perform a soul retrieval. My client gave me permission to attempt this particular healing journey. In my journey I saw that the right side of the client's neck and shoulder seemed traumatized and isolated. I asked this isolated portion of the client's body if it wished to reconnect with the client. The soul of the neck and shoulder gave consent to do so and I returned the soul part to the client. Since she asked me what I discovered, I told her about the soul part that was now reconnected. The client then reported that two days before our session she was in an auto accident and the whiplash hurt the right side of her neck and shoulder. She said she had been so busy after the accident that she hadn't yet had time to process the experience and found this fascinating.

Psychopomp. I've had occasions to perform psychopomp journeys in which an individual or group of traumatized human spirits linger in the Middle World after death and then ask, when given the opportunity, to be guided to their next stage of life. Usually I do psychopomp work in response to Jesus when I have asked him in a journey if he has something he wishes me to do.

Such was the case in early 2017 when I visited Jesus and asked him if I could be of service. He told me to call Phoenix to help me and follow. Phoenix, one of my helping spirits, agreed, and I flew on her back to where Jesus had traveled in the Middle World. I was now in Aleppo, Syria in a bombed-out area. A family of four stood, dazed, in a street near the rubble of a building. There was a grandfather, mother, a young teenage son, and a pre-teen daughter. (The father was not there and I sensed that he was away fighting.) They were all very shaken up and disoriented. I introduced myself and asked them if I could help.

The grandfather tried to talk, but was not very coherent initially. I asked him what he last remembered. He said they were all together in their home when there was a large bomb explosion. I asked them if they had seen their bodies after the explosion. Everyone but the mother remembered leaving their body, but they all felt the need to stick together. I asked them to look up at the sky and see what they noticed. A Light opened up and they wanted to go to it, but were concerned about leaving behind the mother, who was still alive. I asked the mother, Ashia, if it would be all right for them to go. She grieved hard, but she gave her permission and they all said their goodbyes.

Phoenix and I accompanied them toward the Light and when they saw those awaiting them they went on by themselves. We returned to the mother. I assured her that she would meet them again later and asked her about her beliefs. She said that she believed in Allah. I asked her Higher Self if it would be right to ask for a representative of Allah to be with her to give her healing and strengthening light. Upon her permission I asked for a representative of Allah to come to her. A strengthening light then surrounded her and she seemed comforted by its presence. I asked Jesus if there was anything else for me to do. He said I could leave, and I then did so, with Phoenix taking me back to the Meeting Place.

During a walk on the bay trail later in the day I further debriefed the situation with Jesus and Phoenix. I was told by Jesus that I had done what I was supposed to do to fulfill this mission. I mentioned that I was surprised that the situation involved more than psychopomp work, but also included healing for the living mother in her spirit form. I also asked Jesus about staying in the background during the psychopomp work. He told me that he was there if I needed him, and that he gave me this mission to help me gain experience. His compassion, of course, is for all humanity, regardless of beliefs. But Jesus felt it was important to let the mother determine her own way of connecting to the help of the Light and the Holy One.

Compassionate Depossession/Spirit Release. Some clients have come to me with a concern that they or someone they care for may have an unwanted spirit or spirits attached to them or afflicting them. I explain that I am responsible to create a setting that assures the safety of my client. I will determine, with the assistance of my helping spirits, if there is an unwanted spirit entity or entities influencing the client. Then the afflicting spirit is engaged for the purpose of removing it and sending it to a place where it cannot cause further harm, and also has the possibility of undergoing healing and growth in the Light. Both the entity and the client are suffering on some level, and so care (with clear and firm boundaries) is also given to the entity. In this step the client *may* have a passive or active role in engaging the afflicting spirit, but I am the one that directs any conversation with the entity.

I can do spirit releasement work without the conscious participation of the client in the depossession session as long as consent has been given. After the possessing or influencing entity is removed and relocated I work with my helping spirits to clean and heal areas in the client that have been affected. Other shamanic practices for healing might be included in this or subsequent sessions.

THE DARK AFFLICTING SPIRIT

In one case I had previously met with a client whose adult son was also supposed to accompany her for some healing work. She said that her son wanted to come, but was too tired at the time of the appointment. She had concerns that her son was being afflicted by a spirit. I worked with her alone that time, but also got permission to do a remote session around her concern for her son after being assured that her son gave permission for me to work on his behalf.

In the subsequent remote session Bear, along with Archangel Raphael's help, took me to visit the son. Bear was well merged with me. After I finished with a related healing procedure, I asked Bear and Raphael if there was any spirit presence influencing either the mother or son. Receiving a clear response that there was an unwanted entity affecting the son, I asked for the help of the Beings of Light to illuminate the area, which was in the mother's house, where the son also lived. A nonhuman entity emerged. It looked like a gargoyle.

I asked its name and it gave me an unintelligible name, so I told it I would call it "Mikey." I asked Mikey if it was human and it said no. I asked it how it came to be with my client(s). The answer was a bit confusing. Either it had been attached to a friend of the son and jumped to him, or it was aligned with a dark entity that was attached to the friend of the son, it became aware of the client's son, and then started drawing on his vitality. I told Mikey that he could no longer stay with the son since it was harming him, and it did not have the son's permission. But I told the spirit that I could arrange for it to go to a place where it can grow to become truly happy.

I got the spirit in touch with the light deep within it; then with its consent I called on angelic beings to take it to the Light where it could move on. Before the released spirit left, I asked it to repair any damage it was able to for my client and her son. In this situation the compassionate depossession work was remotely performed and without the participation of the clients, except for their consent.

THE MISPLACED FAERIE

I've learned firsthand that occasionally spirits need to be removed from an area that they wander into without any intention of causing harm. Such was the case when I made a personal retreat at the (ordinary reality) monastery where I am connected as an oblate. It is the community's practice to have about twenty-five minutes of silent meditation in the abbey church immediately following Vespers. So I remained for meditation. I went into a shamanic state of consciousness and asked for any of my spirit helpers to come that had something to teach or show me. Melchizedek appeared as a dark robed presence. It may be that his presence was prompted by a psalm that was chanted during Vespers that mentions him. Then archangel Sandalphon appeared, again clothed in a dark robe.

I asked them if there was something that they wanted me to see, thinking that there might be other spirits in the chapel. I then saw, with increasing clarity, standing quietly on the left aisle in the monk's choir section, a spirit that appeared dwarf-like and about four feet tall. It had a large and long nose and a large mouth. It had a blue tunic and a red cloak. I understood that this spirit was a tempter for the monks—a spirit that would prompt gossip in the monastic community. I called upon angels of light to surround the spirit, which happened immediately, and asked my helping spirits how it could be removed. Sandalphon instantaneously whisked it away to a place appropriate to it. (If I were in this situation now I would try communicating with the spirit and seek its permission to voluntarily go to a place more appropriate to it.)

At Vespers' meditation two days later I again entered a shamanic state of consciousness. I set my intention to meet with St. Benedict, the sixth-century author of the monastic rule bearing his name. The ordinary reality monastery merged with my nonordinary reality Monastery and St. Benedict appeared before me in the abbey church. I had met him several times before, but wasn't sure he remembered me. He was of sturdy and medium build, with short curly white hair and a curly white beard. He was dressed in a monk's habit. I greeted him and identified myself. He was friendly and warm, speaking fondly of the brothers at the monastery and commending them for their faithful witness. He said that he knew it was not an easy life and that he keeps watch over them and sends his spiritual support and power to them.

I asked Benedict about the spirit that was at the church two days before that Melchizedek and Sandalphon removed. Benedict was aware of that spirit and said it was a form of faerie folk that lived in the woods in the region and had wandered into the church. It wasn't inherently a dark spirit, but by its particular nature it would have the negative effect of promoting gossip, which would be a vulnerability of some monks and could cause significant harm to the community. It was good to have it removed and sent back where it belonged.

THE "OLD MAN"

In another situation involving spirit release work I met with the client face to face. He was an ongoing spiritual direction client of mine who decided to come for a shamanic healing session with the possibility of spirit release/compassionate depossession since he struggled with a long-standing urge that he feared had the power to derail him. There was some possibility that this was a form of being that had an ancestral/family influence and legacy going back to the trauma of Jewish holocaust experience. In the consultation journey Jesus was the principal guiding spirit for me. I noticed something hovering around my client's head. Jesus counseled that I first perform a spirit animal retrieval to boost my client's power and spiritual defenses. Then I was to conduct a depossession of the "Old Man." I reported this to my client and he agreed to the process.

The spirit retrieval went easily and I brought back to my client a beautiful, powerful animal spirit. I then gave my client various possible ways that he could be involved in the spirit release work. He chose to try to enter a light meditation state and envision the entity. He would listen to the spirit's answers to my questions and relay them to me. In the spirit release work my client saw a two-dimensional, cartoon-like head of an old Hasidic Jew. It was not so much a "man," and the spirit didn't identify as human. Perhaps the spirit was a "thought form" that had been passed on over generations. Yet, the spirit didn't offer a preference for a name so I continued to use the name "Old Man." He was very reluctant to speak and so there was a lot of preliminary silence. I made an assurance of my responsibility for the well-being of the spirit as well as for my client before the spirit began to speak.

My client also needed to be coached to just say what came spontaneously rather than put filters on assessing who was doing the speaking. It later became apparent when it was the Old Man and when it was the client who was speaking. The main concern of the Old Man was the increasing loss of the old Jewish cultural values and arts. Yet he acknowledged that he shouldn't force this on my client. I affirmed it wasn't ethical to be attached to my client without consent and it did my client harm. My client also stated that he felt empathy and even some personal identification with the values the Old Man was so desperate to keep in the world.

I led the Old Man to a vision of his own self being filled with divine healing light. Then I directed him to look above and he saw many of those he considered kindred spirits surrounding the Light. The Old Man briefly conversed with my client, who came to some agreements with him, and then I directed the Old Man to go toward the Light and his spirit friends who would take him to the Upper World. There he could be further healed and then perhaps be able to work with people in a way that is not anxious and controlling, but as a helping spirit. He then left to move on to the Upper World. In subsequent conversations my client reported no longer having any concern about a negative influence underlying his relationships.

THE TRIO OF HUMAN SPIRITS

In a fourth situation I met with a client via a video media platform. She is an ordained Christian minister and also has some experience in shamanic practice. When she was a young girl she was abused by a Roman Catholic priest, and as an adult she gathered some clergy companions to help free her from spirit afflictions associated with the abuse. Recently she was experiencing some concerns and felt she could benefit from a fresh "clearing." After a brief extraction we moved to explore possible spirit release work. She decided to move into a meditative state. I had my healing spirit team of Jesus, Bear, and Archangel Raphael present to do our work. We ended up engaging three discarnate spirits: an old man who died in the 1930s, who attached to her in 1974, a young man "Danny" who was twenty-two years old and shot by a sheriff's posse in the late 1800s, who attached to her when she was seven, and a fetus. The emergence of these entities had come to her as a complete surprise.

I asked the old man, who appeared to be in his 80s, to remember the moment of his death. He was rocking on his front porch, then stood up and grabbed a railing, and then died. He said he liked the client when he came upon her and that was why he attached to her. After working with him and insisting that he must leave to go to a better place, I asked him who he wanted to take him to the afterlife. He was met in the Light by his grandmother.

Danny remembered that when he was hiding in a stable, he heard horses and gunfire. He was holding a white bag of coins that he had stolen. I offered him the chance to take a shower in the Light to remove any remnants of greed or guilt. He saw his horse in the Light. I asked an angel to accompany him. He said he was sorry to my client and asked forgiveness before going on to the Light.

After Danny left my client heard a heartbeat and then saw

the fetus. I invited her to have any conversation she needed with that spirit either aloud or silently. It was a quiet and deeply touching moment. She reported afterward that she said she was sorry and that they could meet again when she transitions to the Upper World. I asked her to call a helping spirit to act as the fetus spirit's psychopomp. The helping spirit then came and gently took the fetus spirit to the Light.

I forgot to ask the discarnate spirits to make any repairs before leaving and so I checked with my client. She said that the old man left some holes in her heart region where he was grabbing on. I went back with Bear and Archangel Raphael to work on filling in the holes and repairing her power and sealing the areas. No spirit associated with the initial abuse came up and apparently the initial ritual fashioned by my client and her colleagues had done that work satisfactorily.

In subsequent conversation with this client, I discovered that the greatest difficulty she had was the struggle to accept that actual release work and healing, rather than fantasy promptings, had happened. Coming from the same culture that denies such realities, I can certainly understand the difficulty in claiming such an experience as authentic.

VISITS WITH DEPARTED SPIRITS

I have already mentioned using the Living Room in the Mansion to meet with departed human spirits on several occasions, and described how I led someone in a guided imagery meditation to help her say goodbye to her father. There have been other situations. I have visited ancestral spirits on various occasions; visiting in the Upper World some grandparents, my adopted father, and most recently my mother.

I'd like to share two visits I made to my mother. The first time was I physically present with her when she was still alive but in a comatose state near death. Physically she had the rapid eye movements I associate with a REM dream cycle. Her physical gestures appeared to be more in response to an otherworldly realm than to ordinary reality. I used a drumming recording on my mobile phone and headset to move into a shamanic journey while sitting next to her. I called on spirit helpers to guide me to her spirit. Jesus, Phoenix, and Bear showed up and took me to her—in a dark and shadowy place (the Interworld zone).

I could see her, but nothing beyond her. She did not seem to be in any distress. I told her that it is nearing time for her to let go and make her journey to the next world. I offered to take her, with the help of my spirit friends, to the threshold of that world; or, she could wait for the Light and be met by others who would help her cross. She said she would wait. I asked Jesus and the others if someone could come from the Upper World to stay with her while she waited for the Light. Immediately Mom's own mother came from the Upper World to be with her. The next day my mother gently died a few hours after her parish priest gave her an anointing and we said a brief litany for those near death. At the moment of her death I said the prayer, *Commendation at the Time of Death*. It felt like I had witnessed a holy death.

Three days later I again made a shamanic journey, this time with the intention to visit my mother in the Upper World. I went to my Meeting Place and asked for Jesus and Phoenix. I asked Jesus if I could see Mom to find out how she is doing on her journey. Jesus asked Phoenix to take me to see her. We went to the Upper World to a city there and landed at a room in an apartment complex. The apartment seemed a little spare, but nicely furnished. Mom was there, was glad to see me and gave me a hug. She appeared to be full of life and vitality. Her age didn't seem to be fixed but varied in appearance from her mid-30s to her 70s. She said that her new life is wonderful and she is now doing an orientation program. There will be lots she can do but she can still be aware of us in our lives and visit us in our dreams and in other ways. She wants us to know of her love for her family, just as I expressed our love for her. She had a particular message for one of my brothers that I passed on to him in ordinary reality.

I used a certain amount of discretion about who in the family I would share information with about these shamanic visits. Some family members are open to the positive and hopeful vision these journey visits exhibited, even if they are understood in different ways. Others would likely be uncomfortable or closed about shamanic practices generally and would see this suspiciously. I understand that this is a real stretch in our culture, even if it is not so in other cultures.

DISMEMBERMENT AND REMEMBERMENT

I have had occasions where, in nonordinary reality, my spirit body has been taken apart and then reassembled by my helping spirits. The first occasion was very early on in learning how to make shamanic journeys. I journeyed to the Lower World and called for Bear and Lion. I was very unfocused and frustrated that I couldn't maintain my vision. I expressed my frustration and asked for help. Both Bear and Lion used their claws and teeth and set to tearing me apart. I was surprised but I did not feel any pain so I simply observed what was happening. Then I had the feeling I had been put together again. After that journey I did seem to be able to focus better. I had previously read about experiences of dismemberment by a guardian spirit animal as an initiation into shamanism so it didn't take me completely off guard.

Much later I made a shamanic journey with the intention of going through a dismemberment/rememberment process. Lion met me in my Sacred Meeting Place and I requested this gift. Lion asked me why and I explained my intention that this would further help me be more fully integrated, spiritually whole, and better connected to all. Lion then took me down with a bite on the neck, and carefully began the process of shredding my flesh and removing my body's organs. Bear came along and joined in the dismemberment. My body became skeletal and the bones were scattered. I thought of the Ezekiel passage of the valley of dry bones. Brother Wind swept around my scattered bones and Bear and Lion then started reassembling my body. Then flesh was built back up. I felt myself whole again and stood up. I saw Lion and Bear standing next to me. I saw that my body was now radiant and luminous. I thanked my spirit friends and affirmed my connection to them, to Spirit, and to all that is.

Death and rebirth is a spiritual theme that shows up in various religious traditions. In Christianity it is a key element of the faith: Jesus' suffering, crucifixion, and resurrection. In that tradition we may make it a spiritual practice to consider the little deaths and rebirths that occur in our lives as Easter moments, times when we face the need to let go of aspects of our life in order to receive the gift of a renewed life.

It is also consistent with the wisdom of dreams where death occurs. In a dream's metaphoric logic something has to die in order for something new to emerge. The price of change is death to the old, but the promise of change is a new life. The shamanic nonordinary experiences of dismemberment and rememberment are akin to this deep wisdom.

CURSE REMOVAL

Situations may arise where a curse needs to be removed as part of healing and restoration work. The following story is likely to be considered a coincidence and I have no way to prove that the results happened, in part, because a curse was removed. But here's my story:

I spent 17 years living in Evanston, the first suburb of the Chicago Northside. If you are a baseball fan and live on Chicago's Northside you are most likely a diehard Chicago Cubs fan. And most Cubs fans know about the famous "Billy Goat Curse." In 1945 at the fourth game of the World Series in the Cubs' Wrigley Field Stadium, the owner of the Billy Goat Tavern, William Sianis, brought his pet goat, Murphy, and was asked to leave, presumably because of the goat's odor. Sianis was infuriated and yelled, "The Cubs ain't gonna win no more. The Cubs will not win a World Series so long as the goat is not allowed in Wrigley Field." The Cubs lost to the Detroit Tigers that year and the curse continued to plague them. The Cubs had not won a World Series since 1908.

I was living in the San Francisco Bay area in 2016 when the Cubs again won the National League Pennant and were set to advance to the World Series. I was still a Cubs fan and supported the "lovable losers." Much talk was stirred up about the Billy Goat Curse as the Cubs advanced to the World Series. I wondered...could I help the Cubs by evening the playing field? It had been over 100 years since the Cubs won the World Series. Haven't they suffered enough? Don't they deserve a real chance to win?

I made a journey to Bear and asked for help. Bear took me to the Billy goat (Sianis's goat Murphy) and we all journeyed to Wrigley Field. Bear, Billy goat, and I walked across the field to the home team dugout and went down to meet the Cubs' team players. The team petted the Billy goat and welcomed him to the stadium and apologized for their refusal back in 1945. That ended the journey. I took it that the curse was removed. The Chicago Cubs were free to win or lose the series on their own merits without a curse handicapping them. And the Cubs went on to win the World Series for the first time in 108 years.

A MEDICAL CRISIS AND HEALING JOURNEY

I had a medical crisis that initiated a personal healing journey that included both Christian and shamanic healing practices. So I want to share this story as an integration of the practices I have described throughout the chapter.

At the end of August 2017, I had a major health crisis involving lower GI hemorrhaging that required three blood transfusions. Western medicine's language for the episode is that arterial bleeding erupted in an area of my colon where there is a large amount of diverticulosis, and it eventually resolved itself. My experience is much more nuanced. I deeply appreciate that the medical care I received kept me alive over the week of hospitalization and saw me through the eruptions of bleeding. But I also want to add my gratitude for the various forms of spiritual medicine that I received that made this medical crisis a profound healing journey.

I have often heard people in my faith community remark on how important the prayers of friends, family, and community members were to them when they were in an acute health situation. That, too, was my experience. To know that I was being prayed for, or that "healing thoughts" were being sent my way, was spiritual support that was almost tangible. I felt held up and surrounded by love and care.

One of my priest colleagues happened to be a chaplain at the hospital where I was receiving treatment. He visited me and my wife several times, offering me steady warmth, openness, and a solid understanding of how patients are treated. Both of the staff priests at my parish came to see me, offering authentic care, listening presence, and the sacramental rite of healing.

During the period of my hospitalization and the days following my return home, I made several full shamanic journeys and also some brief conversations or visualized scenes with my helping spirits. When I was in hospital care I felt even

more permeability than usual between ordinary and nonordinary reality, reminiscent of Celtic notions of "thin space," and it
was easy to move into a shamanic state of consciousness.

The first formal shamanic journey was by a meditation on
the first night of hospitalization. I envisioned going to the
Monastery and asked the monks and nuns to admit me to their
Infirmary. I was taken to a bed there. I felt relief that I was in
sacred space, where the care of God's healing power and love
would be available. It was a short meditation, and I soon lost
focus, but felt comforted.

The second journey while I was in the hospital was much
more intense and focused. I began at the Meeting Place and
asked my spirit friends to join me at the Healer's House. I flew
there and entered. The inside of the house, normally a modestly
furnished place, was transformed into a large surgical-type
room. The Healer appeared as a being of light. I lay down on a
steel table. I was surrounded by many of my spirit helpers,
including Jesus, Lion, Bear, and the archangel Raphael. Bear,
who is often my partner in shamanic healing work for my
clients, leaped up on the table. I looked down from above at my
body and saw Bear carefully, with intense concentration, paw
through my small intestines, and then move down to my colon.
Bear then removed a spirit intrusion that appeared to me as a
cutworm. Bear plopped the intrusion into a basket we use to
contain and remove intrusive spirits, and then whisked it away
and immediately returned. As Bear was taking away the intrusion Raphael cast a radiant healing power over my lower
abdomen.

I had hoped that the bleeding would be over following this
spirit healing intervention, but that wasn't the situation. In the
next two days I needed to receive three transfusions of blood,
and I was feeling discouraged and began doubting the effectiveness of the shamanic healing I had received. I felt like I was
approaching the Interworld zone and psalms of distress were

coming to my mind. It was a comfort to share my discouragement and concern with a priest colleague, my wife, and one of my brothers. I then began to gain perspective.

I remembered that in shamanism a classic initiatory journey often occurs during a life-threatening health crisis. Perhaps what I was undergoing in the spiritual dimension was just such an initiation to a new level of shamanic ability. In a brief divinatory meditation I called upon one of my spirit teachers to advise me. He reminded me that Bear's and Raphael's healing was not necessarily immediate. Often it takes days or longer for the shamanic healing to fully manifest, and how it manifests is not always predictable. Also, shamanic healing sometimes requires multiple sessions. But I also was given an assurance that the bleeding had stopped. That knowledge grounded me again. I was less anxious about the unknown.

I also sent out an email to a couple of colleagues in shamanic practice asking for help. One shamanic practitioner replied soon thereafter: "Daniel, I did a journey for you. Saw you surrounded by a circle of bears who offered you healing & protection. Sang you two bear songs. Keep me posted." It was comforting to learn that my shamanic practitioner friend saw bears offering their care, and it also felt like a confirmation of the work Bear was doing for me.

Two days later I was able to go home and I continued my recovery, but not without a further moment of alarm. On my sixth day home I passed a large blood clot. I had been cautioned to go to the ER if I was passing copious amounts of blood. This wasn't a sign of fresh bleeding, but it was a disappointment. I felt angry and ready to fight this condition and return to good health. I called on my Bear and Lion friends to equip me with their fierceness.

I then did another formal shamanic journey. I went to the Meeting Place and called upon all my helping spirits and teachers. I saw many of them individually as they came and packed this gathering area. I told them of my recent bleed and how much I wanted to fight for my health, but I needed them to help me. We decided to go to Healer's House again, back to the large surgical-type room. I got on the table and Bear again started going through my gut looking for further intrusions while Lion safeguarded me. Bear removed another smaller "cutworm" intrusion and cleansed and repaired and sealed the area with Raphael's help. In the meantime Melchizedek and Raphael scanned my lower chakras and my aura and repaired and sealed areas that were weakened. Raphael and Jesus then renewed the protective and powerful spiritual radiant luminosity that, like a transparent outer shell of an egg, surrounds me. This was the last major shamanic journey I needed to do over the course of my recovery to health.

REFLECTIONS FROM THE HEALING JOURNEY

The most frequent description of Jesus' earthly ministry in the gospels is that of bringing healing to those in need. Healing sometimes resulted in cures, sometimes not. Healing is a broader category of graced action and can be carried out in non-physical situations as well as applied to physical conditions. There can be social, psychological, and spiritual dimensions to healing, and Jesus' ministry touched on all of those. Jesus proclaimed that healing was a sign that the kingdom or realm of God is close at hand.[6] From a Christian perspective, this wholistic approach to healing—and offering resources that support multiple interactive dimensions of healing—is an extension of Jesus' healing ministry in our time. From a shamanic perspective, it is evidence of the presence and love of compassionate and highly evolved spirits that desire to bring help, wisdom, and healing to our troubled Middle World. As we apply the gifts of healing grace to people in need, trusting that

God's compassionate power and presence is near, we become participants in God's healing work.

In the course of this healing journey I now know my spirit friends more intimately and trust them even more deeply than before this crisis. I have worked with them before in shamanic healing for others but now I've felt their gentleness, power, and care directed at me. They are all representatives of God's love and compassion, but they are also their own "persons" and want growing relationships with me, as I do with them. This is an amazing wealth of relationships that most of us are ignorant of, or hesitant to explore and develop, given the strong influence of our Western rationalist culture.

The final fruit that I pass on to readers is to invite each of you to reflect on your own ways of participating in this expanded understanding of healing and the vastness of the healing community. We can all take our place in God's movement towards health and wholeness. In these healing and discernment opportunities we are not alone. There is a vast company that desires and is ready to assist us, so vast that our best imaginings cannot contain them all.

6

GOING DEEPER

A Q & A WITH OUR READERS

THE WORLD OF SHAMANISM

*W*hen you have these shamanic experiences, where are you? What are you doing? For example, are you just sitting or lying there somewhere with your eyes closed? Or are you physically acting out the scene? Or are you just walking around, doing whatever, going about your regular business of living, while all this is going on inside you? Or something else?*

Katrina: Shamanic experiences can occur in many different ways, although there are certainly common practices. What is core to all of them is the opening to "nonordinary reality" (NOR) so that the presence of spirits can be perceived (seen, heard, felt, or sensed in any way). Typically, and especially for someone new to shamanic practice, the experience does indeed involve lying or sitting down, with eyes closed. This is usually done in a quiet place, without interruptions from "ordinary reality," to allow the person to be fully present in the realm of spiritual reality.

However, dropping into awareness of NOR, and connecting to spirits, can happen in any context. Dancing, maybe with eyes half-closed, is a common mode of journeying into the spirit world. Drumming while one journeys is also common. I believe Daniel discusses walking while connecting with his spirit helpers, and this is a favorite of my own as well. Doing sitting meditation also may evolve into a shamanic journey, if I allow myself to be open to that. I even remember my first teacher of shamanism telling me how her spirits would help her choose vegetables to best nourish her family, as she shopped in the produce department of the grocery store! When one is open to the presence of spirits, listening to what they may be offering, their presence can be found in any number of times and places.

Daniel: There are parallels between shamanic practice and some Christian prayer and meditation practices—which is not too surprising since they both involve opening to nonordinary reality, as Katrina states. There are the formal practices that are learned and cultivated. These condition us to open to the spiritual realities that are part of life.

In Christian tradition we can learn particular forms of prayer and meditation, such as saying the Lord's Prayer, or reading the Daily Office, or joining in congregational liturgical prayers, or spontaneous verbal prayer. We might also view stories in stained glass windows, or sing chants, or pray with icons. Then we might learn about Ignatian meditations on scripture stories or scenarios and practice them. Perhaps we begin integrative prayer and meditation practices like *lectio divina*. We might intentionally practice "seeing" Christ/Divinity present within another person and treat the other as bearing a sacred dignity.

We are learning to shift back and forth from "left brain" verbal and mental prayer to "right brain" forms that engage visualization and feeling levels; shifting from "head"-based practices to those that flow from the "heart." As we grow in our capacity and pick up experience and awareness of being helped by God's grace and spirit friends, we increase our ability to weave prayer and meditation and/or shamanic journeying more fully into our life.

I'm fascinated with this idea of three levels of existence in shamanism—the Upper, Middle, and Lower Worlds. How do those track to the Christian "map" of Heaven, Purgatory and Hell?

Daniel: I wrote earlier that I think of the shamanic Upper and Lower Worlds as dimensions of the Christian concept of Heaven or paradise. The Upper World is easier for Western Christians to grasp as corresponding to Heaven, but there are differences even there. In shamanic worlds, this is the location of saints, angels, other angelic hosts, and many deceased relatives. But this is also the dwelling of various teachers beyond a conventional Christian understanding of who gets to go to Heaven, and it is also the place of legendary and mythological figures, gods and goddesses.

The Lower World is like the nature-focused dimension of Heaven with its animal beings and powerful plant and elemental beings. It is the likely place of choice for people to go who are drawn by their indigenous culture or intense love of nature. That, too, can be a stretch for a Western Christian orientation that has associated the lower regions as the places symbolically located for Hell, Limbo, and Purgatory (depending on the branch of Christianity). Making shamanic visits to the Upper and Lower Worlds will challenge conservative salvation beliefs and may stretch even a universal salvation theology.

Core Shamanism avoids belief statements (unlike culturally or religiously-rooted shamanism) and instead encourages direct experience in the nonordinary worlds. There does not appear to be a place that corresponds to a Christian notion of Hell in all of its gruesomeness. However, many shamanic journeyers report that some areas of the Interworld regions of the Middle World have a purgatorial or hellish feel to them, where there is suffering, depression, despair or hopelessness, and bleak darkness. I've made some psychopomp journeys with helping spirits and Jesus where human souls were released from very dismal Interworld situations. The humans had been filled with shame and unworthiness and were fearful about moving on, afraid of judgment, until our visits.

Many modern Christians view Hell no longer through the medieval symbols of wrathful judgment, torture, and the devils, but as a spiritual and emotional state of deep suffering and death through our rejection of God's ongoing offering of grace and love. So too, Purgatory might be understood as our Middle World experiences of suffering in the process of being transformed with the help of God's healing love and grace. Purgatory could be understood as a spiritual and relational state of cleansing and purification with divine help.

For some the language of directional locators (up, down, in, out) on a "map" might get in the way if we think of it concretely. To the modern mind, Heaven is not literally "up there." Hell is not literally "down below." Neither are the "Upper" and "Lower" worlds necessarily up and down. These are limited directional and locational symbols used to help us visualize directing our consciousness to spiritual dimensions of reality.

John: It might help to keep in mind that, in the Christian tradition, Heaven, Hell, and Purgatory are thought of as eschatological ends or destinations, whereas the Upper, Middle, and Lower Worlds are more like England, France, and Spain—on a map, England sits atop France and Spain, but it isn't any better than France or Spain (the British may disagree...). These are just regions of activity where people are alive and active now (not having reached some kind of eschatological fulfilment). These regions are different from one another, just as England is

different from Spain. Maybe I'm making this more convoluted?
(Laughs...)

RELIABILITY AND SAFETY

In what way are shamanic experiences "real," and what makes you
think you can trust them? Are you really interacting with spiri-
tual beings, or is it something in your imagination—or is that one
and the same? If the experience is just being generated within
yourself, how is it valid or useful?

Katrina: Yes, what *is* real in this realm of spiritual experience? How do we know what reality really is, and what dimensions of reality may exist beyond our perception and possibly
beyond our conceptual ability? This question is so relevant to
how we relate to any part of our religious or spiritual beliefs,
regardless of our affiliation or identity.

Within the arena of spirituality and religion, we may choose
to believe in any number of things for which we have no "proof"
within the current scientific paradigm. We cannot know what
the reality of these things may be, but we do know that our
experience of them is real. We can welcome the gifts of the
experience whether or not they are "real" (within a particular
definition of what reality is). Even if one believes that the events
of a journey are entirely from the imagination, and that the
imagination is just a part of the self, they are a gift from beyond
our conscious mind that offers us more than we can access
through our normal consciousness.[1]

Michael Harner distinguished between ordinary reality (OR)
and nonordinary reality (NOR), as Daniel previously discussed.
In this framework, events in journeys or other shamanic practices are real within NOR—not real in the same way as this
chair I sit on, but real on another level. We can enter into that
level of reality without fully understanding how it exists, and
have deeply meaningful experiences with spirit helpers, just as

we can pray to a God who is beyond our ability to understand or perceive.

As far as safety is concerned, there are guidelines for practice that help ensure the safety of a person's experience. Core Shamanism teaches that all beings on certain levels of NOR are compassionate, with the desire to assist humans, and all events there are beneficial. Working within those guidelines is important, and this speaks to the need to have some training or mentoring, or at least solid study in this area.

Another thing that Michael Harner said is actually the simple answer to all these questions: It is not a matter of belief, but rather just a matter of experience. One can believe or not believe in the reality of any of this, but if your experiences are powerful and beneficial, you will see the work as valuable and worthy of continued practice.

How is shamanism different from divination or occultism or sorcery? Doesn't the Bible condemn such things? Isn't it inconsistent with Christian theology?

John: Divination, occultism, and sorcery are different things, so I'll address them separately. Let's talk about occultism, first, shall we? The word "occult" as we use it is fairly modern, and it is not found in scripture. The word simply means, "not visible," "obscured from view," or something that cannot be seen. By that definition, anything spiritual, including God, is "occult."

As for divination, the Jewish and Christian scriptures do not speak with one voice on this issue. The Jewish scriptures speak of the Urim and Thummim, two stones that resided in the breastplate of the high priest (Exodus 28:30). When the clergy needed to determine the will of God, these stones were removed and probably rolled like dice (Deuteronomy 33:8-10; 1 Samuel 10:22; 2 Samuel 5:23). In the Christian scriptures, the

Acts of the Apostles tells us that the disciples cast lots to determine God's will about who should replace Judas among their number (Acts 1:12-26). There are other instances as well—see Genesis 44:1-5, Numbers 5:11-31, Judges 17-18 for more instances where divination is portrayed in a positive light.

The most unequivocal condemnation is to be found in Deuteronomy 18:9-14, especially verses 10-11, "No one shall be found among you who makes a son or daughter pass through fire, or who practices divination, or is a soothsayer, or an augur, or a sorcerer, or one who casts spells, or who consults ghosts or spirits, or who seeks oracles from the dead." The key to understanding this prohibition, I think, is in the beginning of verse 10, where it refers to the sacrifice of children.

This was the primary abomination, an abhorrence that echoes throughout the Jewish scriptures, from Abraham's aborted sacrifice of Isaac, to the various prohibitions on mimicking the behavior of the "nations" (gentiles), including witchcraft and other "magical" practices. The two are linked in the ancient Jewish imagination. "Don't be like those people who murder their children, nor do anything that they do," seems to be the sentiment.

I think this sentiment is one that we share, and I don't think those of us who are exploring shamanism are in any danger of child murder, which is the real objection to such practices.

Finally, let's discuss sorcery. Sorcery is commonly used to refer to so-called "black magic" in which demons are called up and coerced to do the magician's bidding. This is very dangerous stuff and never to be attempted. First of all, it is never a good idea to involve yourself with demons, unless you are an exorcist getting rid of them. Demons are bad. Demons are malevolent and dangerous. I believe demons are real and that no one should willingly have anything to do with them. Did I mention they were dangerous? Besides, while it's rarely a problem to ask spiritual beings (including angels) to do things for you (this is called "prayer"), binding them to your will is coercive, and therefore incompatible with the Gospel.

Are you likely to encounter demons in shamanic practice? It isn't common, but I wouldn't rule it out. What is common is to encounter spirits in the Middle World that are up to no good and that do not have your best interests in mind. But that is why the discernment of spirits is so important in this work. Exorcism is also a very common shamanic practice. But often, in shamanism, even the malevolent spirits have a positive role to play in our healing and liberation. That may be true of demons, too, in an ultimate, expanded view that we cannot comprehend. Let's leave that to God.

The main point I want to make is that the kind of practice you encounter in shamanism is not coercive, does not invite congress with demons, nor does it advocate the ritual murder of children. What the Bible condemns has little in common with what Core Shamanism promotes.

Daniel: That's a brilliant explanation, John! The only thing I want to add is that not all shamanism is non-coercive or avoids sorcery. Some cultures have fierce rivalries between shamans where sorcery is part of the mix or where a shaman can be hired to cause harm to a targeted person. Core Shamanism, which we are presenting, eschews those practices and may at times provide healing for victims of sorcery.

Jesus says, "Take heed that no one deceive you" (Matt 24:4-5). How can you find a shamanism teacher you can trust?

Daniel: For a Christian, Jesus (or the Holy Spirit) is the primary teacher. Go to him in prayer or meditation and ask him to help guide you to a trustworthy shamanism teacher. Like spiritual guides and spiritual directors, there are many shamanism teachers who offer their services. Training programs, including the Foundation for Shamanic Studies, often list people who have completed different levels of their program in a directory with contact information. You can interview some prospective shamanic practitioners or teachers and get a sense of the way they would work with you. Ask them about how they would work with someone who has a religious faith. Ask about how they stay accountable to high standards of practice. Be prayerful about this and listen for the Spirit's guidance about the choices before you. Do a similar discernment process if you are seeking a training program. You may want to write or speak to an organizational representative about your questions.

THE DISCERNMENT OF SPIRITS

How do you know the spirits you're dealing with are good ones, "angels of light" rather than "angels of darkness" (2 Cor 11:14)? If demons are real, might they not use the journeys to deceive you? Can you talk about the discernment of spirits?

Daniel: If you have any questions you can test the spirit (1 John 4:1) as to its true nature. In Core Shamanism there is always the freedom to take the advice of a spirit or not. We are taught that the Upper and Lower Worlds are the regions where compassionate and highly evolved teachers and helpers can be found. The Middle World spirits have their own needs and may have less altruistic motives. But there is nothing wrong with questioning any of them to see how compatible your basic values and core understandings are with the spirit you are encountering. Is what the potential helping spirit saying or doing consistent with the "fruit of the Spirit" (Galatians 5:22-23)—love, joy, peace, patience, kindness, generosity, faithfulness, gentleness, and self-control? Does this spirit bring healing, wholeness, and wisdom to situations in a way that shows God's shalom/peace? If you are a Christian, you might want to seek Jesus' or Holy Wisdom's guidance about the nature of the spirit.

John: That's good advice. I'd like to add that, if encountering a spirit in the Upper or Lower worlds, I'd be inclined to take them at their word. I would still want to see if our values were compatible, as you suggest, Daniel. But I wouldn't assume that they might be lying to me. The Middle world is different. You can test the spirits in the Middle World, too, but I'd take their responses with a grain of salt. They may very well be out to deceive me, and I would take that into account.

Daniel: John, I think your inclination is sound. I don't feel the same need to carefully discern spirits in the Upper and Lower Worlds as I would in the Middle World. I've learned by experience that these are "safe" realms. In the Upper and Lower worlds I have met spirits that are not interested in me; they are focused on other things, or they redirected me to see another spirit. But I've not met a spirit there that gave me lasting concern.

I was once taken to Asclepius, the Greek god of healing who also appears as a serpent, on a higher level of the Upper World. He offered to be an ally for me in certain healing situations. As a general rule, if I am thinking of working with a spirit from the Upper or Lower World, I check for their attitude about me being a Christian and the importance to me of the partnership I have with the spirit of Jesus. I did this with Asclepius, who respected my conditions. We have since worked together in some healing situations.

In the Middle World I have very friendly relationships with many nature spirits. But some are upset (justifiably) because of how we humans are mucking up the environment or encroaching on their traditional territory. It's with humans (deceased or alive!) and other highly sentient spirit beings that I feel the need to be especially discerning. I make it a rule when journeying in the Middle World to always invite the company of my tried-and-true helping spirits to accompany me. They can provide protection and offer counsel about the spirit in question.

Katrina: Following these good points you both make, I'd like to add another, about the perception of "safety" with spirits, or lack thereof. As may have been evident in some of the stories in the book, the work we do with spirits often may appear a bit frightening or threatening in its form. It may, in fact, *feel frightening*! So much healing work on the shamanic realm involves breaking apart or dismemberment of some part of ourselves, physically and otherwise. If we perceive this as it would be in ordinary reality, it's scary! It may also be disturbing to our ego-structure, as the shamanic healing may threaten well-entrenched and familiar patterns or beliefs we hold. This disruption of our personal status quo could be experienced as "unsafe" if it is held without trust in the helping spirits and without the willingness to allow ourselves to be broken apart and re-formed, psychically speaking.

Are the forces that are from outside oneself (referred to as demons in the book) specific to the person? Where do they originate? Does a person (perhaps unknowingly) do something to bring about a particular "type" of demon? Are certain people attracted to certain types of demons?

John: Okay, let's talk about demons, shall we? (Chuckles.) Demons are not really an optional part of Christian cosmology, although a lot of Christians these days would like to think so. I remember hearing about someone who came to their pastor to inquire about an exorcism, only to be told there was no such thing as demons, and was given a referral to a psychologist instead. Sigh…

Of course, many conditions that might feel "demonic" are psychological conditions, and even some of Jesus' encounters with demons in the gospels sound an awful lot like mental illness (Luke 8:26-39, for instance).

Okay, I just had to get that out of the way. But assuming many demonic encounters are *not* psychological issues, scripture actually isn't very clear about just what demons are or how they work. We can extrapolate from the stories of Jesus' encounters with them, but the fact is that scripture just doesn't say that much about them.

We learn a great deal more about demons from literature within the tradition, such as the Desert Fathers and Mothers, for whom battling demons in the wilderness was a daily affair, and a bit like hand-to-hand combat. They spoke of demons as forces exterior to ourselves that nevertheless attack us from an interior place—in other words, through temptations.

Now, "temptation" is kind of a fusty, old-fashioned word these days, but it's an important one, in my opinion. We face temptation every day, we just don't often think of it as such. I remember once I was agonizing out loud over whether the book I was writing was "absolute crap," and whether I should scrap it and start over, and my wife held up her hand and said, "That's a temptation." Suddenly everything snapped into place. I was able to see that I was being attacked by thoughts that sought to undermine my work, thoughts that were not necessarily mine. This is a very common occurrence.

This is not demon possession, of course. Instead, it is a mild form of demon *oppression*. And while demon possession is exceedingly rare, demon oppression is exceedingly mundane. So when you ask, "Are the forces that are from outside oneself specific to the person," I'm inclined to say no. We are all being tempted to undermine and hurt ourselves and others, pretty much all the time. Somehow, most of us are also given the grace to resist these attacks. What *is* specific to each of us is the particular ways that we are likely to be tempted.

When one of the monks complained of demon oppression,

one of the Desert Fathers replied, "When the demons sow bad thoughts in you, have no truck with them, for they are always taking the initiative. They never miss a chance, but they cannot coerce you; the choice is yours, whether to accept or not... Do not answer when they begin to speak. Get up and pray; make a prostration saying: 'Have mercy on me, Son of God.'"

St. Ignatius said that "the evil one is like a military commander attacking where one is weakest" (Spiritual Exercises 327), which suggests not a distinction or specialization among demons, so much as an opportunistic approach to attacking where people are most susceptible to temptation.

We really get the idea that there are types of demons (and along with these types, specializations in temptations) from medieval grimoires like *The Lesser Key of Solomon*—which is kind of a bestiary of demonic rulers and the specific varieties of temptations and sins each demonic dignitary specializes in. I'm not aware of a text closer to the orthodox center of the faith that would support this system of categorization. If anyone knows of one, please share, because I'm interested!

So, the shorter answer to whether there are certain kinds of demons that specialize in certain kinds of temptation or sins is...I don't know. It makes sense, but I'm not aware of evidence in the tradition with any kind of proximity to scripture that would support that. The closest thing I can think of from scripture is where Jesus says that certain kinds of demons can only be driven out by prayer and fasting (Mark 9:29). Jesus is making a distinction among demons on how to drive them out (or the difficulty in doing so), but not really about types of temptations or sins associated with them.

Daniel: Some forms of Christian deliverance will refer to the "demon of..." and fill in the type of sinful oppression (lust, wrathful anger, drunkenness, etc.). Francis MacNutt often names the demon that way. That may be confusing the demonic spirit with the kind of symptom the person is experiencing.

In core shamanism the label "demon" is avoided and instead there is a preference for "dark and powerful spirit" to provide distance from any religious belief system. Shamanism is highly experiential and I cannot say I have encountered a demonic spirit in shamanic work—yet. But I am not ruling out those beings, however we might name them or however they might name themselves.

I have encountered situations where the sense of evil was palpable and my suspicion was that the person was under the influence of a demonic spirit. My sense is that these are opportunistic beings that are moving in due to a person's vulnerabilities.

The distinction between full-blown possession and oppression are helpful, John. Maybe a third category of demonic "obsession" could be added? Demonic obsession is the earliest of the stages, where temptations are growing so strong that they are undermining the person's life. Many forms of demonic interference are experienced as involuntary takeovers, but a person could voluntarily make a contract with a demon/dark spirit in order to get a particular benefit from the relationship. That will not end well.

John: (Thinks for a minute.) You know what? I don't think I'm done yet. Sorry to be so verbose! (Laughs.) But I think this is important. I think it's problematic for us to mix-and-match worldviews when we are talking about shamanism and Christianity. They really do posit two different universes, and these universes are mutually exclusive places. This is true of any two religious systems, not just these two. If you are going to enter the Shamanic universe, you have to accept its worldview and play by its rules.

Imagine a long hallway, with doors on either side. Go into any door and you enter a different universe. That's the way it is with religions. Those of us who do interfaith work have to develop a kind of paradigm-surfing muscle, so that we can enter a string of mutually exclusive universes in quick succession with minimal vertigo. It isn't easy and it takes some practice!

One thing I've learned is that it isn't helpful to mix apples and oranges. It makes no sense to enter the Shamanic universe and expect to encounter Christian or Buddhist personalities or phenomena. So asking, "What about demons?" when talking about shamanism is a bit like asking, "Can Buddhists go to heaven?" It's the wrong question. Buddhists have no interest in the Christian heaven, and the Christian heaven has no place in their universe. There are no demons (as Christians define them) in the shamanic universe. Scratch that—there are only demons in the shamanic universe if I bring them with me. I'm holding that passport.

I think there's a difference between how Daniel and I blur those lines, but in both cases, I believe, we are each responsible for the ability to blend them. I use shamanic techniques to navigate in the Christian universe, whereas Daniel enters the shamanic universe, but encounters Christian personages like Wisdom and Jesus. My personal opinion is that Wisdom and Jesus don't actually live there, but that Daniel brings them there, and uses the shamanic universe as a forum for his encounter with them. Perhaps that amounts to the same thing, but I think it's an interesting and important distinction that bears more thought.

I'd be interested in what you think of that, Daniel. Also, Katrina, do you ever encounter Buddhas or Bodhisattvas or figures from non-shamanic traditions in the shamanic realm, and if so, how did they get there? Did you bring them or are they somehow residents? Or am I trying to be too literal about what is essentially a mystery? That might be, but I don't think it's out of line to ask the question.

Katrina: Certainly not out of line to ask the question! Actually, I do see it differently, John, and I share some of Daniel's experience of the crossing-over of cosmologies. I believe, and have experienced, that the shamanic realm includes beings from all arenas of spirituality or religion—and a shamanic-type experience can occur whenever one encounters a spirit teacher from any tradition. In the Interspiritual view, which I share, all of these manifestations of the Divine that we categorize into different faiths come from the same source, and are accessible to all of us. Within a shamanic journey, who would say that Jesus or Krishna or Buddha is not able to show up or is not welcome?

My own experience may add more here, as I do come from an open spiritual background. Over the years, a handful of teachers or helpers have shown up who surprised me in their self-identification. (I am always hesitant to share names but you did ask…so I will try this to see if I want it so public). One of the earliest spirits who showed up was Isis, not by me invoking her or even in any way having a particular connection to her. Possibly she is a *different* Isis, not *the* Isis…but it does not feel so. More recently, maybe three or four years ago, I began to be accompanied and held by a man with big white wings who then identified himself as Michael. Is he the Archangel Michael? I don't know—but again, this came to me unbidden, possibly from a tradition with which I have had very little personal experience.

Similar, but a bit different, were meetings with two powerful religious figures while I was learning about their respective religions at The Chaplaincy Institute. First was during my practice of Christianity, taken on to deepen my understanding of this faith that was somewhat foreign to me. In my morning practice I began to say the Lord's Prayer, repeating it many times. At one point, I was clearly "visited" by Jesus and had a powerful experience of him connecting and holding me, specifically, in his love. For a length of time, his presence as a spirit helper was part of my spiritual life. Was this Christian practice, or was it shamanic? A similar thing occurred when I was in the Hindu

Temple, at the feet of the blue Vishnu. As I knelt in the shrine that was not of my faith, with which I had almost no familiarity, Vishnu made himself palpably present with me. None of these appearances were evoked by my history nor intention, but I see all of them as evidence of the power of those spirit entities and their desire to help all beings, regardless of affiliation or theology.

Daniel: John, I may have thrown you off when I wrote that I think of the Upper and Lower Worlds as heavenly realms. They are not the equivalent of a Christian universe, nor do I have the sense that I am importing personages from a Christian universe into a shamanic universe. But I wonder who made it a rule that the "universes" have to be mutually exclusive? Maybe the shamanic "universe" is far vaster and incorporates, not imports, elements of religious universes.

John: Fascinating! I'll have to think about that.

Daniel: That is closer to my experience from my own journeys. But I do have some Middle World "constructs" that originally were developed in my expanding Christian universe (Monastery, Wisdom's and Healer's houses, and Mansion) and are functional in my shamanic universe. Maybe there is a dynamic in the shamanic universe that both personalizes our experience and also stretches us.

Michael Harner wrote about the surprises Westerners experienced in looking for a teacher in the Upper World: "Persons first visiting the Upper World are often surprised by the identities of teachers waiting for them… Here in North America, members of the Christian clergy often found their teachers to be ancient Greek and Egyptian deities, Native Americans, or Hindu saints, a result that most seemed to accept. In other words, there commonly was an ecumenical aspect to their experiences. Likewise, agnostics, atheists, and Jewish visitors are frequently surprised to find that their teacher is Jesus or a Christian saint."[2]

I found that to be the case. My first Upper World teacher was a Native American from whom I still draw wisdom and healing. Asclepius, an ancient Greek and Roman healing deity, is a helping spirit for me. But I am also in relationship to spirits from Jewish and Christian traditions. I have teachers in the Lower World too that are not, so far, from the Judeo-Christian pantheon of saints. But who knows who I'll meet in the future? Harner, who did not profess a religious faith, didn't seem to see this as a case of Christian importation into the shamanic worlds, but rather that all kinds exist there in a nondogmatic way and we get to be surprised by the vastness and mystery. I know that I am!

SHAMANIC EXPERIENCES

Have I not had experiences like this because I lack imagination?

Katrina: Not at all! Whether or not you have had these kinds of experiences is a factor of something like temperament as well as intention. I know wonderfully creative and spiritually deep individuals who have tried to journey but had nothing happen except a deep meditation to a drum beat. For some reason, there are some individuals for whom this form of spiritual practice does not fit. We might theorize about the reasons for that but it is not a lack of imagination nor spiritual commitment.

On the other hand, if you are wanting to have these experiences but cannot seem to get there, sometimes a helper can facilitate that. Having clear guidance about how to move into shamanic reality or take a journey can clarify the intention and thus make possible the experience. Not always, but sometimes, this support can help the person have an experience they would not have had otherwise.

Daniel: I think there is something like the imagination's "muscle" that needs to be exercised in order for journeying to become a memorable experience. When I was first attempting shamanic journeying, I wasn't able to get much of a sense of the nonordinary world. Images were very scant and hazy. I felt discouraged and wondered if I was cut out for this path. But over a series of journeys I began to gain more clarity about that world. In a similar way, those who persist in recalling dreams— even if they are slight fragments at first—are likely to see their dreams grow in vividness over time. So if at first nothing or very little appears to happen, do not give up right away. Another thing to consider is that some of us are more visually oriented, but others may discover that another sense (hearing, smell, taste, touch) is dominant in a shamanic journey, or that an intuitive feeling state has been activated.

Katrina: Yes, I think the awareness develops so that we begin to perceive more of what is present when we journey. And I also believe that, for most of us, the world of the spirits begins to somehow make itself more accessible when we persist.

I'm interested in the contrast between Christian "faith" and the direct spiritual experiences shamanism affords. What is the role of faith in shamanism, or direct experience in Christianity?

John: Ah! You've hit upon one of my favorite soap-box issues. "Faith" in Christian teaching is problematic, because I think we essentially misunderstand the word. The word for "faith" in Greek is *pistis*, and it can mean intellectual belief (or assent) or emotional trust. Greek is often a more precise language than English, but this is one of those cases where they have only one word and we have two, and the distinction between them is pretty important.

When most Christians hear "For by grace you are saved through faith" (Ephesians 2:8) or Luther's more concise, "We are saved by faith," our knee-jerk response is to assume it means intellectual assent to the set of metaphysical propositions set out in the Apostles' or Nicene creeds. But that's not what it means at all. A much better translation is "We are saved by trust," which has nothing to do with believing a bunch of abstract ideas, but everything to do with heartfully trusting this person, Jesus.

And you only learn to trust someone when you have an experience of them. You trust someone because you experience them as trustworthy. So I consider the "faith" vs. "direct experience" dichotomy in this question to be a false premise. Christianity does not require abstract belief from us—well, some forms of Christianity might, but God does not. True faith (by which I really mean trust) only arises because of direct experience and requires direct experience.

I'm not saying that any Christian who has not had a direct experience of God isn't a true Christian, but I am saying that I consider such a faith to be anemic. A profound and robust *pistis*/faith/trust requires a direct experience, a resting-in, a letting go of intellectual notions in favor of a raw, real, experiential relationship that alone can mediate substantive transformation/divinization/*theosis*.

Can shamanic practice help a person have this direct experience with Jesus/God/the Holy Spirit? Absolutely...which is why this interests me, and why I find it useful. Especially since it helps people sidestep centuries of execrable and obfuscatory Christian teaching to get at the real enchilada.

But I don't think shamanic practice is the only way to get there. There are plenty of tools/techniques/disciplines within the Christian tradition that can get you to the same place. But because I think we've become numb to some of the practices in our Christian tradition—or worse, forgotten about them—I think shamanic practice holds promise as a way to shake us out of our dogmatic torpor, to help us access that direct experience.

Daniel: Well stated, John. There is the "faith of the Church"—teachings that provide an understanding or worldview drawn from history and scripture. That can continue to develop as we discern the guidance of the Holy Spirit in our present situation as a Church. But there is also the concrete lived faith experience of people and communities, drawing upon prayer practices and forms of meditation that seek a direct relationship with God. In my opinion, many church leaders fail to adequately teach their people these dynamic ways of prayer and meditation. The tools are there in the greater Christian tradition for direct experience with the Divine. Shamanism offers other tools for direct experience of spiritual realities.

SHAMANIC PRACTICE VS. CHRISTIAN PRACTICE

Some of Jesus' actions and teachings seem vaguely shamanic. Was Jesus a shaman?

Daniel: There is good evidence to suggest that Jesus fulfilled all the roles in his society that would be ascribed to our present understanding of a shaman. The most convincing arguments I've read are by South African scholar Pieter Craffert in his book *The Life of a Galilean Shaman.* Craffert argues that it is probable that Jesus would have fulfilled the entire cluster of societal roles that his world associated with what we now call a shaman; and that many of his actions in the gospel stories were understood in his culture as work through nonordinary reality that a shaman would access. That is not to say that he was limited to that role.

John: There's that apples-and-oranges thing again. I think we need to be careful. I think it's important to say that Jesus was *not* a shaman, he was a rabbi, and that he did not understand what he was doing as shamanism. *And* at the same time, many of the things he did remind us powerfully of things that shamans do, and may have fulfilled some of the same functions—and gotten some of the same results—that shamans do. It's helpful for us today to draw parallels and make comparisons—compare and contrast!—but at the same time we must be careful not to project things onto Jesus that he would not have recognized as his.

Daniel: It seems to me that Jesus would have understood himself to be more than a rabbi/teacher. An obvious point is that his ministry included being an agent of God's healing. There were itinerant wonder-workers in his world. Would he have recognized that role as a part of who he was? I agree that there was no particular word for shaman in his culture, but that doesn't mean he didn't have an understanding of himself that included, but wasn't restricted to, what we might now think of as shamanic. Maybe it isn't apples-and-oranges as much as tangerines-and-oranges? At least in the same citrus family (smile). John, you are right that we should be careful what we project upon him. And, Lord knows, we have projected all manner of things onto Jesus—much of which he might not own. How do we get inside Jesus' own self-identity? Maybe we ought to ask him, what do you think?

John: Ha! I have often said that Jesus may or may not have taken upon himself the sins of the world, but he certainly bears our projections!

Is speaking in tongues a shamanic practice?

Daniel: Yes, just as tongue-speaking (glossolalia) can occur in the Christian religious context, and in other religions, it can also occur in shamanic practice. But there are differing forms of glossolalia. While I have witnessed lengthy ecstatic utterances in Christian charismatic circles, sometimes followed by an interpretation, I have not experienced this among shamanic practitioners.

Making animal sounds is not unusual when a shamanic practitioner is merged or working with a particular animal spirit. I have been present at shamanic gatherings when a person who is merged with a spirit sang a brief song or chant in an unknown language to a group.

Receiving a song conveying healing power or taught by a spirit to invoke its presence is a common practice. In my experience the focus has been on receiving the song and then spontaneously singing it—with or without words. Often the song is conveyed by simple vocalizations. I have later added words to some songs (tunes) I received from particular helping spirits.

John: I would love to hear some of those! I'll bring the wine, Daniel, if you'll bring the songs.

Katrina: Related, but somewhat different, is the occurrence of a shamanic practitioner speaking in the language, accent, or voice of a spirit being with whom they are merged. I have seen only a little of this—but I have been told that it does all happen.

If I have Jesus, what need do I have for other "spirit helpers"?

John: This is a very Protestant response! You might as well ask, "What need do I have of community? Of role models? Of other people at all?" There's a tendency in Protestant spirituality to go into a "just me and Jesus" mode that isn't really healthy. Besides, "need" for what? For salvation? If by salvation you mean a shield from the wrath of God, then I'll leave you to it. But that's a pretty narrow definition of salvation, one that distorts the divine image, and not one that reflects the depths of our tradition.

Here's how I understand salvation in the Christian tradition: Because of the cumulative damage of human sin, everything we love (or should love) is broken. Our relationships with God are broken, our relationships with other humans (from individuals to nations) are broken, our relationships to the earth and our fellow creatures are broken, and even our relationships with our deepest selves are broken.

The eschatological promise of the gospel is that, in the fullness of time, God will heal everything broken—everything, everything, everything. This understanding of salvation sees all of creation as being in communion and community—a communion that is currently compromised, but the restoration of which God is actively working toward—as are we.

This is why we gather around the Eucharistic table every week. The Eucharist is a participation (in the now) in the fulfillment of all things (in the then). This fulfillment makes no sense in a "just me and Jesus" kind of spirituality. The universe is a community. The doctrine of the Trinity reveals that God is a community. Jesus is the one who calls us into community. Community is salvific, because what we need to be saved from is not God (and "his" wrath) but isolation and brokenness. Community heals (at least healthy community does), and so, by definition, community is salvific. A bowling league can be salvific!

It is from the perspective of this Christian theology of brokenness and redemption that shamanism speaks to us so powerfully. Shamanism pulls back the veil to show us that our community is much bigger than we thought. Not only are we in community with other people, but with those who have gone before, with "angels and archangels and all the company of heaven," as Daniel has already mentioned, with spirit guides and chthonic creatures, all of whom are acting in the interest of our healing and wholeness.

Shamanism reveals that all of creation—not just physical creation, but the vast world of spirit as well—loves us and cares about us and is guiding us beyond brokenness into right relationships with all things, creating healing in all four directions —healing those relationships with God, with each other, with the earth, and with our deeper selves.[3] It reminds us that we are not in this alone, but are part of a vast cosmic dance of interconnection and communion. Jesus is a part of this, certainly, but as a Christian, I believe that all of this is a gift that Jesus (as creator, John 1:3) has given to us. Why would we reject such a gift? Especially when that gift is itself the healing, the salvation, that I am most in need of and that God has promised?

Katrina: John, I love your answer here, especially your final points. Yes!

Daniel: In a narrow sense, you don't need helping spirits if you have Jesus! But you cut yourself off from all of God's other messengers and helpers and spiritual kin. Do you refuse the help sent by God through an angel? That isn't a very biblical response, is it?

Katrina: Indeed, we need all the help we can get! And there is also the strong possibility that the "medicine" offered through one helper will be different from that from another—or that we may be differently able to receive from diverse sources. Just (ha!) as our bodies need multiple vitamins and minerals, and best absorb them under different conditions.

Catholic spirituality interacts gleefully with those on the "other side," praying for and to the dead, while Protestantism eschews such practices. Can shamanic practice help Protestants directly access the profound riches of the Communion of Saints?

Daniel: There are spiritual practices that have been carried on through the Catholic side and the Orthodox side that can benefit Protestants and help them live more deeply into the possibilities of the Communion of Saints. Having been raised in Disciples of Christ (Christian Church) and American Baptist traditions, the concept (theological doctrine) of the "Communion of Saints" was foreign to me. It wasn't until my late 20s and a move to the Episcopal Church (a "bridge" between Protestantism and Catholicism) that I was introduced to the Communion of Saints—that God holds all the saints, living and dead, in love as a great relational community.

Through prayer and meditation we can continue to be in relationship with the departed through the loving grace of God. Since prayer and meditation are relational activities rooted in God's love and care, we can continue to be in communication with the departed "beyond the veil" as well as those who are alive in this world. The *Sanctus* in the liturgy of the Eucharist, as John pointed out in his chapter on Christianity, celebrates that Communion of the Saints where we join in prayer and song with "angels and archangels and all the company of heaven" in giving thanks to God.

Catholic and Orthodox traditions have what I think of as portals to the nonordinary sacred realms to help focus and open up our relationship with saints and Jesus. Catholic statuary and crucifixes and Orthodox icons can be powerful visual aids to prayer and meditation that help us in prayer to access in nonordinary reality the presence of saints and angels.

So in returning to the question of whether shamanic practice can help Protestants directly access the riches of the Communion of Saints, it seems to me that there already are shamanic elements in the broader faith tradition that point to the benefits of such practice. I've already described some of the shamanic journeys that I have taken that profoundly deepened my relationships with saints and deceased loved ones. My previous experience with meditations, using the visual tools of Catholic and Orthodox traditions, helped prepare me to make shamanic journeys and to more fully engage God's beloved community on the other side. Protestants are not the only ones who could benefit from shamanic journeys to visit the saints and those known to us on the other side.

SPIRITUAL HEALING

What do you mean by "healing" in this context? Are there certain types of people who are more amenable to spiritual healing? Are there people who are more resistant to it?

Katrina: When we speak of healing, it may refer to various forms or dimensions. Healing is distinct from curing an illness, although all parts of the self may need healing for something that manifests as physical illness. Healing may be on the level of physical illness, and also on the psychological or spiritual levels. Sometimes healing has nothing to do with the body at all.

Within shamanic practice, the form of healing can look different, depending on what is sought, but different "treatments" may be needed for different aspects of the person. Some practitioners just focus on healing the body through work in the spiritual realm. Others may focus more on the psyche of the person (healing old traumas or harmful beliefs, for example) and others may focus just on spiritual malaise (repairing soul loss or helping the souls of those who have died, for example). These approaches, of course, may be combined as needed.

While there are not categories of people who do or do not benefit from shamanic healing, there is one factor that certainly affects whether the healing is successful: whether or not the person truly wishes for healing. In some cases, a person is attached to the state of dis-ease or illness, for some reason (often unconscious) and there is resistance to letting it go. Or, the malaise may be caused by an underlying psychic aspect that the person is not able or willing to look at or change. Naming and addressing that resistance may be necessary before healing can occur—indeed, that process of addressing resistance is in fact part of the healing!

While each of us may hold different definitions of exactly what health and healing look like, the healing work of shamanic practitioners is done with awareness of the interconnection of body, mind, soul, and also the wider field of spiritual reality. For each person seeking shamanic healing, the path of healing and the methods of the practitioner will depend on the exact needs of the person.

Daniel: I've thought a lot about this question over the years. I appreciate Katrina's response and concur with her view of shamanic healing. In regard to Christian spiritual healing, there are some things we can learn from the gospels about how Jesus practiced and taught. In some areas many were healed by Jesus, but in one locality he marveled at the people's lack of faith, and few people were healed. In one situation the person, who was blind, needed a second touch by Jesus for the healing to be complete. Jesus warned that if a person is delivered from an unclean spirit, that person should adopt healthy spiritual practices to safeguard against the invasion of demonic spirits. He told his disciples that some tough cases of exorcism require fasting and prayer.

These gospel situations and teachings point to some limitations on healing. Some healing doesn't happen immediately and may require a series of spiritual healing sessions. Faith—that is, an active trust in God's grace and ability to provide health and relief from suffering—is a necessary component. A person seeking healing must not be a passive recipient but actively participate in working toward new health and well-being. And there are some cases that require more than is apparent at the time, perhaps other spiritual disciplines either by the practitioner or the person asking for healing. The particular healing practitioner may reach his or her limits of ability and someone else may be better suited to the situation and the patient, or a team of practitioners might be required to work together. Besides these considerations, sometimes other things need to happen before a person's presenting need can be adequately addressed. And sometimes, as St. Paul learned from his own experience, living with an affliction is part of what gives witness to God's sufficient grace.

I hear you saying that the images that come to you in journeys/visions/dreams have healing power, but I don't understand why that would be. Can you explain how and why that happens?

Daniel: It happens because the images that are seen in such special journeys/visions/dreams are not mere fantasy appearances. These images carry about them, or point directly to, the substance of a spiritual reality that is not normally seen but still affects us. These journeys or visions or dreams present powerful, dynamic symbols (but "symbol" is inadequate; so too is "archetype") that work for healing or bring new wisdom and understanding to a situation. These images are our visualization of alive, powerful beings that we call spirits; beings with autonomy, power, and compassion that can interact with us.

Katrina: I want to echo Daniel's perspective on the healing power of images found in shamanic work, and expand it a bit. I agree that we don't have a sufficient word to express the power that these "images" hold. It is almost like the image is a coalescence of healing "energies" (a word that Harner did not allow!) and those energies are conveyed and released through the awareness of the image. Just yesterday I noticed the healing power of an image that a client had been given in a journey and then contemplated regularly. The "image" was not a helping spirit but an occurrence, an interaction. The healing image may in fact be conveyed through other, non-visual senses such as a vibration, a sensation, a song or phrase, a place, an element, or a force of nature, to name just a few. The form the image takes is a specific prescription for the individual seeking help, with the healing power inherent in the form it manifests.

Daniel: Our book is replete with examples of how these helping spirits can work with us for our greater health and well-being. Let me give another example related to the Christian practice of the healing of memories. A person is emotionally troubled over something that occurred in the past and in a visualized meditation asks Jesus to accompany her to the memory of the past event that was so painful. Suddenly the event is recalled, re-lived through visualization, but now Jesus is there in the midst of the past event alongside the hurt person. The person can talk with Jesus and see what Jesus does in the event. In the re-lived situation Jesus brings to the sufferer new understanding, insight, comfort, or support. The person now "knows" that she was not alone in that traumatic moment and a reframing of the meaning of the event occurs. There is healing power in that journey into the past accompanied by the spirit presence of Jesus.

Since our bodies, minds, emotions, and spirit all interact as a whole system the healing impact of the meditational journey may not only provide emotional relief, but also might bring a positive change to the person's physical health and well-being, create opportunities for some personal relationship changes in a healthy direction, and deepen her sense of spiritual peace and relationship to her God.

Can shamanic practice provide an antidote for the void of meaning in contemporary life, or even alleviate our terror of death?

John: I think that most forms of religion and spiritual practice can help us find meaning, in that it connects us to something larger than ourselves. The word "religion" after all, comes from the Latin *"re-ligion,"* which means "to connect again" or "to reconnect." Something has become disconnected—we have become isolated and somehow cut off from a larger story that gives the smaller stories of our lives context and meaning and, therefore, hope.

As a Christian, I live inside the Christian story, in which the smaller story of my own life makes much more sense, and allows me to place my small efforts into the context of the much larger movements of God acting in history to heal the world. By myself, I'm not contributing much to the whole, but as a piece of a much larger puzzle, I see that my piece is important.

I think the crisis of meaning in our culture is due, largely, to the fact that, as more and more people have left traditional forms of faith behind, they no longer see their small stories as being part of a larger, meaning-making narrative.

Secularism has done a lot of good things for us, but meaning-making isn't one of them. Myths, after all, are stories that make sense of our lives. By devaluing myth and making the term synonymous with "false stories" that are divorced from history, we cut ourselves off from their life-giving, contextualizing power.

When Marcus Borg said, "Everything in the Bible is true, and some of it really happened," he's getting at some of this. There is a way in which story is more important than history, and in our mad dash to discard everything not provable by the scientific method, we have gleefully traded our souls for fool's gold. Myth tells us the truth about our lives, in a way that is truer than history. This is related to the distinction between the chapel and the living room that I talked about in my earlier chapter.

I think that one thing that shamanism can do for us is to provide a means to connect with the spiritual world again—with myth and what I like to call "Big-Ass Story"—in a way that doesn't trigger us, as so many of the religions do, because of our history of discrimination, fundamentalism, and hypocrisy.

I've made my peace with the problematic aspects of my own faith, but I understand why other people can't—or won't, or even shouldn't. Shamanism gives me hope that there is another way that people can connect to the spiritual dimension of life that doesn't necessitate years of therapy and working through mountains of dogmatic nonsense. I'm looking to shamanism for other reasons, but for those who are turned off by the so-called Big Religions, there's a lot of potential there for real, vital connection with a spiritual reality, and the hope of discovering a Big-Ass Story that can give someone life.

Katrina: Yes, I see shamanism as an open invitation to engage with the Divine, in ways that may speak better to many individuals. The practice of shamanism may be more palatable for some in this time of popular rejection of "Big Religion" in that it does not have much of the baggage that religions seem to now carry—or be perceived as carrying. Also, that direct connection, that multi-sensory *experience* of spiritual presence, can cut through the intellectual objections that may block some from religious participation.

Daniel: I want to focus on whether shamanism can alleviate the "terror of death." I had several meditational experiences prior to engaging in shamanism that were pivotal in shifting my attitude toward my personal death. In my early twenties I occasionally practiced a Buddhist meditation on observing my body slowly dissolve into the elements. Then, in my seminary clinical pastoral education I came across Simonton's meditation on envisioning our death and asked my supervisor to lead me through that journey from nearing death, dying, envisioning my funeral, and then reviewing my life before the divine maker of the universe. The unexpected and immense love I experienced from the Holy One was so powerful that I didn't want to return to this ordinary world!

There were other experiences that shaped my attitude toward my mortality that dispelled the terror of death before I began my shamanic exploration. However, in my shamanic journeys, I have visited deceased loved ones and experientially envisioned where human souls go in their normal passage after this life. So, I think that shamanism can help us peer beyond this mortal veil and dispel the fear of death. But I also think that positive religious prayer and meditation practices, along with living life with loving intensity, can help do that as well.

Poet Robert Bly wrote this version of a poem by the fifteenth-century ecstatic religious Sufi/Hindu mystic, Kabir:

> *Friend, hope for the Guest while you are alive.*
> *Jump into experience while you are alive!*
> *Think...and think...while you are alive.*
> *What you call "salvation" belongs to the time*
>   *before Death.*
>
> *If you don't break your ropes while you are alive,*
> *do you think*
> *ghosts will do it after?*
>
> *The idea that the soul will join with the ecstatic*
> *just because the body is rotten—*
> *that is all fantasy.*
> *What is found now is found then.*
> *If you find nothing now,*
> *you will simply end up with an apartment in the City*
>   *of Death.*
> *If you make love with the divine now, in the next life*
>   *you will have the face of satisfied desire.*
>
> *So plunge into the truth, find out who the Teacher is,*
> *Believe in the Great Sound!*
> *Kabir says this: When the Guest is being searched for, it*
>   *is the intensity of the longing for the Guest that does*
>   *all the work.*
> *Look at me, and you will see a slave of that intensity.*[4]

Katrina: I love Kabir's/Bly's words here, and so relevant... which makes me think this, in response to the original question:

Maybe shamanic work helps to dispel the fear of death through the breakdown of the perceived duality of body and spirit? "... What is found now is found then..." As we come to know that spirit is inherent in all of physical reality, the disconnect between life and death is lessened. This, of course, can be found through other spiritual traditions as well, but shamanic practice is a particularly potent way to encounter this perspective.

BEING A SHAMAN

Does one choose to become a shamanic practitioner, or is it something that is, in a sense, intrinsic to a person? Is it something someone can develop or create within oneself, or is it something that a person either has—a "gift" of sorts—or does not have?

Daniel: I think many people are hard-wired with the capability for becoming a shamanic practitioner. But having the basic potential is not enough by itself. I think something like a "call" from beyond our self that is met from deep within our self is part of the process—whether suddenly or gradually experienced; coming out of a crisis event or unfolding from the direction of someone's life experience. Those of us living in the dominant Western rationalist culture do not receive the same encouragement, community discernment, and access to teachers for becoming a shamanic practitioner that traditional shamanic cultures provide. And remember that only a few people in traditional cultures become a shaman. It requires dedication, and it can be costly. There may be an element of having a gift for this, but it needs to be cultivated and trained (by capable teachers and by our spirit allies) to develop our potential as practitioners.

John: Daniel, you make an important point when you remind us that only a few people in traditional cultures become shamans. You don't need to train as a shaman to benefit from shamanism, or to go on a shamanic journey, or to incorporate techniques into your spiritual practice. That would be like saying you need to become a spiritual director in order to pray! Having a shaman as a spiritual guide and mentor can give you lots of tools and support, and may be all that many people need to access the treasures that shamanism provides. Only a few are called to become "professionals," but many can benefit from its teachings and methods.

Katrina: Yes, and I think we are in an interesting time with this question. As you say, John, many can benefit from the practice! I think the sharing of that knowledge is being called forth at this time as humans explore increasingly diverse paths toward Spirit. Although it is the traditional role, being a shamanic healer for others is not the only way to practice shamanism. Some of us now are called to share the teachings with others, to widen the circle of those who directly connect to spiritual reality through shamanism.

Could you each tell the story of how the spirits "chose" you? How did you know there were spirits summoning you?

Katrina: I can't say the spirits chose me, but I certainly was met when I stumbled through that door! As I detailed in my chapter, the circumstances in my life made me a prime candidate for becoming a shamanic practitioner, with a need for a more tangible connection to the great mystery some call God. A "random" comment from a friend at a time I really needed to connect to Spirit led me to my first shamanic teacher, and once I was there it was full-speed ahead. From my first journey, I felt the presence of spirits available to help and that compelled me to keep coming back. If it was the spirits who sent my friend to connect me to the shamanic path, infinite thanks to them!

Daniel: I don't have a specific experience that seemed definitive to being "chosen." It was much more of an unfolding of my spiritual path. Dreams and dreamwork beginning in childhood have always been an important part of that process. Serendipitous situations evoked a sense of the mystical in me and then set me on a path of studying various religious and spiritual traditions. Visualizing meditations and depth prayer experiences further sensitized me to the spiritual realms. Through it all I became aware of a desire deep within my soul to expand my communion with the visible and invisible worlds and to give witness through my exploration and activities to God's all-encompassing love, grace, and amazing creativity.

John: I don't have an experience of being "chosen," either, nor did I feel "summoned." It was a life crisis that first led me to take a shamanic journey, at the suggestion of my psychotherapist (who also practices Core Shamanism). But, like Katrina, when I stepped through the door, spirits were waiting to receive me and teach me. I think this is important, because shamanism is kind of a great equalizer. Yes, some of us feel a call to go "deeper" and receive training, but the spirits are there for anyone who seeks them out. There's no hierarchy of "important" versus "unimportant" people, no "chosen" or "unchosen." The spirits are there for all.

Is there any connection between a person's power animal and their personality? Does the animal select the person, or does the person select the animal, or is some third party involved?

John: I don't know if there's an unseen third party involved —the universe, perhaps? God? Some celestial *yenta* or angelic functionary? Who knows? One thing I can tell you is that the journeyer has absolutely no say in the matter.

As I wrote in one of my chapters, I'm a dog person, so I thought for sure my power animal would be a dog. So when I went on my first journey, who shows up? Panther.

I have no affinity for cats whatsoever. Double that for big cats. I did not choose Panther. Panther chose me. (Or perhaps was assigned to me by that mysterious third party, because Panther didn't seem to be too happy about the match either.)

As for personality, that is also a mystery. I am generally a cheery, gregarious sort, though at turns thoughtful and quiet. But Panther is almost aggressively surly—maybe grumpy would be a better word for it. He is a cat of few words, and what words he uses (yes, he speaks English, when he speaks at all) are blunt, few, and usually acerbic. He suffers no fools. He is not someone I would want to get into a tangle with. He is absolutely nothing like me.

But I also feel he is there for me. He is fiercely protective. He is *scary*. Let's just say I'm glad he's on *my* side.

So, no—I don't think we have any control over who our power animals are, nor do they necessarily correspond to our own personalities—no way, no how. But that's just my experience. Your mileage may vary.

Could you reject a power animal who shows up? Maybe you could, but why would you? Panther has taught me a lot—but that's *because* he's so different from me. I think if I'd gotten the power-animal dog of my dreams, I would not have learned nearly as much about myself.

Katrina and Daniel, what have your experiences been around your power animals? That is, if you feel at liberty talking about them in public.

Daniel: I have permission from my power animals to speak and write about them. That is a departure from more traditional shamanic protocol. Michael Harner wrote that the spirits want us to know that they exist. That is part of the reason why I don't keep them anonymous.

Two spirit animals first emerged from my dreams. As a child I often dreamed of African lions. They were usually in a family group—a pride of lions. I was part of that pride. There's a play on words here because my maternal grandfather's family is the Lyon family. I carry this family name as my middle name. And we are a prideful family indeed. I experience Lion (now visualized as a mountain lion) as capable of helping me in situations where I need to exercise leadership, grace, and confident power. Lion is also likely to offer responses to questions if someone asks for help and guidance. Those responses are often brief, terse, and to the point. (John, a little like your Panther! You can't mess with the big cats!)

Bear, too, first came to me in dreams. Bear emerged when I moved to California in 2009. Bear, fearsome and powerful as it is, gave me gestures of friendship and belonging in my dreams. This power animal has been my most constant companion in situations where healing is sought. Bear also frequently travels with me in new territory in the nonordinary worlds and can guide me to meet particular beings I want to visit. Bear and Lion were the first power animals to meet me and offer an alliance in shamanic journeys to the Lower World. I experience Bear and Lion as my principal protectors and companions in nonordinary reality. I am very fond of them.

Other power animals have been retrieved for me by other shamanic practitioners or have emerged in my journeys to the Lower World. A couple began relating to me in the Middle World. Most have remained with me—taking on specialized roles on my "team" of allies.

Zebra, a very social herd animal, helps me negotiate issues or questions in social situations. Zebra helps me when I need to be invisible, as well as when I need to step up my level of social visibility and interaction. I am by nature a very shy and introverted person so I am grateful for Zebra's help and wisdom. Zebra offers wise and compassionate guidance for others who seek it.

Hummingbird is a delight and joy. Hummingbird often quickly volunteers to help in situations where someone is suffering from depression or other emotional or mental difficulty or a related injury. Merging with Hummingbird and flying around is an amazing experience!

Phoenix is a constant friend and powerful helper when I make journeys to the Interworld or in psychopomp situations. The words to my song for Phoenix are:

> *Do you see me?*
> *Do you hear me?*
> *You call to me,*
> *I fly to you*
> *bringing healing and power.*
> *Death and ashes cannot hold me.*

Other power animals have helped me in particular situations, but are not usually part of my team. Snowy Owl, Eagle, Lamb, Butterfly, and Buffalo come to my aid on occasion. Since this question is about animal spirits, I will simply remind readers that there are other members of my team that are not animal spirit beings (but some of them can manifest, shapeshift, as power animals).

Like John, I have never turned away from a power animal's offer to help, although I know that I could and the animal would not be resentful—they do not have the kind of egoic concerns we humans have. Considering the question of how power animals are selected, I find that they came to me or were given to me, rather than my specifically seeking a particular animal. However, once we are in an alliance, I might ask for a particular power animal's help based on its particular strength and my situation.

Do shamans tend to have certain personality and/or temperament types? What kinds of people are more likely to become (or be)

shamans? Are certain Myers-Briggs and Enneagram types "prone" to shamanism?

Daniel: My first thought was that a shaman is likely to be intuitive, has a lively sense of imagination, is drawn to the spiritual, and has a keen sense of wonder. I shy away from using personality typology for identifying a person as a likely shaman candidate. It feels too limiting for the variety of people that may become shamanic practitioners. But really, I think that everyone has the potential, but it is the Spirit that moves some of us into shamanism.

John: I understand that reticence, but I'm going to rush in where angels fear to tread! My experience is that most people who go into ministry are NF's in the Myers-Briggs system, meaning that on the second continuum, Intuitive vs. Sensing, most people in ministry are Intuitives, and on the third continuum, Feeling vs. Thinking, most people in ministry are Feelers. I'm going to guess that most people who are drawn to shamanism as a spiritual practice are also going to be NF's.

(The first and fourth continua—Introvert vs. Extrovert and Process vs. Judgement—don't matter as much, although probably there are more Introverts and more Process-oriented folks in ministry than Extroverts and Judgement-oriented folks, but I think the contrast is less stark on those continua and that there is more diversity on these poles in ministry).

But let me take Daniel's note of caution and emphasize that I think these types are *descriptive* and not *prescriptive*. What I mean by this is that if you took a poll of people who practice shamanism, the majority of folks are going to turn out to be NF's, but that is not to say that there are no ST's or that ST's can't be or shouldn't be shamans. Just that there will probably always be fewer of them in the mix.

I haven't done a study of this—and I'd love to read one!—but here is my best guess as to personality types who tend to be shamanic practitioners, in order of greatest percentage:

INFP (there are more of this type than any other in the
shamanic community)
INFJ
ENFP
ENFJ
INTP
ENTP
INTJ
ENTJ
ISFP
ESFP
ISFJ
ESFJ
ISTP
ESTP
ISTJ
ESTJ (there are fewer of this type than any other in the
shamanic community)

I myself used to be an ENFJ, but I'm growing more introverted as I age. I am now an XNFJ (X being used to denote
someone more or less in the middle of a continuum). So my
type is about fourth down on the list.

As for the Enneagram, I've never had an affinity for it,
although I usually test out as a 4. But just as there are dog
people and cat people, I think there are Myers-Briggs people
and Enneagram people. I am definitely a Myers-Briggs person. I
can never keep all the Enneagram types straight, and have
found studying it of limited value for myself. But I'd love to hear
someone else opine on this question from an Enneagram
perspective.

Just for fun, Katrina and Daniel, what are your Myers-Briggs
types, just to test my theory?

Daniel: I identify as INFP, so there you go, John! I also identify as a 5 (Observer) in the Enneagram typology. We highly value wisdom and harmonious systems, with a strong 4 (Romantic/Artist) wing. But I hesitate to make any generalizations correlating Enneagram types and shamanic practitioners and do not know of any studies.

Katrina: John, you are on the mark! I am either an INFP or INFJ, not sure which is currently accurate. As for the Enneagram, I seem to be an 8 (Protector) with a strong 2 (Helper) wing. And I wonder too about astrological types, if we are looking from this kind of perspective.

You all have multiple roles: pastor, priest, spiritual director, possibly even friend or family member. You probably bring some of these roles into the relationship with a potential client. How do you distinguish among them?

John: Just as "good fences make good neighbors," good boundaries make for good ministry. Each of these roles draws boundaries in different places, depending on what is needed and what is required for safety. Is it sometimes confusing to remember where the boundaries are when I take off one hat and put on another? Not really, although I am often conscious of it, and sometimes have to think it through. Part of that thinking-through often involves considering how it would be different were I acting in another of my roles. This is helpful for discernment, I think.

The boundaries are probably blurriest in my role as pastor, since as pastor I am often most involved in the lives of my parishioners, whereas I am not involved in the lives of my spiritual direction clients at all, aside from our one hour together per month. I would never visit their homes, for instance, unless there was a case of grave illness, whereas as pastor I am often in people's homes, or at their birthday parties, or at the hospital with them.

Among friends and family members, I am neither pastor, priest, nor spiritual guide! That's a very important boundary. My family needs to go elsewhere for those roles, as I cannot (and should not) try to provide them myself. (Woe to those who try!) When Jesus said, "No prophet is welcome in his own home town," he might as well have said, "No pastor is welcome in his/her own family"— meaning that I am very welcome as husband or brother or father in my family, but I had better leave the collar in my car when I come in.

I imagine it is the same for a shamanic practitioner. Were I to go into that as a part of my professional ministry, I would do well not to try to shamanize with my own family.

Daniel: I rarely bring my role as priest, spiritual guide, or shamanic practitioner into family matters and generally avoid doing so. Since my family has had generations of experience of members who are ordained ministers they are pretty savvy about us being just another member of the family with feet of clay. That's a relief. My wife is also an ordained minister, so while we share many common interests and have an ongoing practice of sharing daily devotional prayer, we have others that we go to for our personal pastoral care and spiritual guidance needs. My wife is curious, and sometimes fascinated, with what I share from my shamanic practice. But she also maintains an interested distance.

Sometimes my volunteer roles in the church get blurred and when that happens I work to clarify which role is fitting. But my church is staffed by other clergy who have formal pastoral responsibilities, so I don't experience the same expectations (and projections) that they do. In my private practice in spiritual guidance, sometimes a client wants spiritual direction and sometimes the client is looking for assistance or coaching in shamanism. We work together to be clear how the client can best be served. There might be some fluidity between spiritual direction and shamanic practice. The late Morton Kelsey suggested two levels of spiritual direction—an ordinary level and a shamanic level.

Our culture is highly professionalized, and generally that is a good thing that emphasizes avoidance of dual relationships. But all of these roles share a common root in serving and supporting the spiritual needs of humanity. That can sometimes mean that as a friend or family member I might bring in something of what I know into the situation. That calls for wise discernment along with love.

Katrina: For the most part, the different hats I wear in my life are kept apart, as Daniel and John describe—I don't wear two hats at once. And yet, there are places where the separation is not so solid. In particular, this is true in the context that Daniel mentioned: spiritual direction work. My directees all know that my primary practice and orientation is shamanism, as this is part of what I tell people who consider doing spiritual direction with me. I do not expect or invite people to engage in that path, and yet there are people who ask to have that included in the work they do with me. In this scenario, I am very clearly not doing shamanic *healing for them*, as that would be a boundary violation or dual relationship. Often, however, I assist them in doing their own shamanic journeys, and help them explore the meaning of the experiences they have. Bringing shamanic work into the realm of spiritual direction in this way can support that person's connection to the Divine—and that is my job when I wear that hat!

I will also say that there are times when I similarly support a friend or family member in that way, by explaining the journey process, possibly drumming for them or even taking a journey on their behalf—*if* they ask. Maybe this is technically a dual relationship, but, as Daniel says, there are moments when it feels right to serve my beloveds with my knowledge, using care and wisdom in the process. This of course is not the same as entering into a client relationship with them!

. . .

How does a client choose you? And how do you decide whether to work with that client? Do people come to you for the wrong reasons?

Katrina: I assume we are talking just about the shamanic work here (speaking of hats...)? I suspect that people come to me for that in the same way as they might go to another: being drawn by the work itself, what I bring to it, and then feeling a sense of trust in our work together. Of course, referrals may have something to do with it, too! Since my work as a shamanic practitioner is primarily in the role of mentor or facilitator, I am happy to work with anyone who wishes to learn the practices. While I can imagine a situation where it may not be appropriate for a person to engage in shamanic journeys, I have not encountered that yet. Part of the beauty of the Core Shamanism approach is that there are safety nets built into the work. I also deeply trust the work of the spirits, that they will show up in the way or the form that best serves the needs of the person I am supporting. I have never seen this fail.

Yes, there may be times when someone may not have a clear or clean motivation for doing this work. This is then part of the discussion before any shamanic work occurs. The discernment process of *why* this work is calling someone is an important element of working with their connection to the Divine, with the broader picture of their spiritual life. If someone is coming for somewhat "wrong" reasons, but there is no danger in that, they will continue on their path unharmed should they not find what they hoped for in the work.

Daniel: In both spiritual direction and in shamanic work I have a little sorting out time with the client. The client has normally come to me by a referral or through a directory, but we typically talk things over to see if there seems to be a good fit between what the client is looking for and what I can provide. I also pray/journey about the client's needs and my ability to work with that person. There have been some times when my spiritual direction work with a client has brought up a particular need or focus for exploration that is best worked with other than through normal spiritual direction. Sometimes a healing need surfaces where focused counseling or psychotherapy might serve the client better or in addition to spiritual direction. Sometimes a healing need has a spiritual base to it that a form of healing prayer or meditation or a shamanic healing practice might address. In those situations I work with the client either directly or by making a referral, again with the guidance of my spirit helpers.

Do some come to me for the wrong reasons? Maybe not so much wrong reasons, but as a shamanic practitioner I've had clients with expectations that I could not meet, or we discovered that there was a limit to what could immediately be done and the person wasn't yet ready to take a longer spiritual journey into deeper healing.

IN CONCLUSION...

Different spiritual traditions have particular gifts to offer for the good of humanity and the world. What are the major gifts that shamanism and Christianity bring?

John: I think that shamanism teaches us that there is a spiritual reality that is concomitant with ordinary reality, that the Otherworld is not far, but is in fact very near. It teaches us that all beings (including spiritual beings) are ultimately here for the healing and wholeness of the world, and are concerned with healing the wounded and fragmented parts of each of us. It teaches us that the universe is trustworthy, that there is a cosmic, divine conspiracy afoot to bring all things into harmony, balance, and health.

Christianity resonates with this grand design, teaching us

that the ultimate end of all things is the healing of everything broken. This is symbolized by the great feast at the end of time that Isaiah speaks about (25:6-9) where none will ever be hungry or thirsty again, and war will be a distant memory. We part the veil of time and make ourselves present at this feast every time we celebrate the Eucharist.

Christianity also teaches us that the Divine is found in the ordinary—that God is found in a human being, that grace is available to us through everyday, sensible objects such as water and oil, bread and wine. It teaches us that God works not through the grand and the powerful, but through the lowly and the common. It teaches us that God's concern is for all people, but that the poor and the outcast have a place of special honor in God's heart—and the implication is that they should have a special place in ours, as well.

As we grow closer to God, we should love what God loves. Martin Luther taught that the work of God in us is the transformation of our self-serving love (which is what we are born with) into self-giving love (which is what God *is*). As we are transformed by and into this kind of love, we will create communities that will transform the world, until all is "shot through" with grace, blessing, and divinity, leading eventually to the healing of all things.

Far from being at odds, I believe that shamanism and Christianity have goals that are not just compatible, but are looking at the same process (and looking toward the same eschatological fulfillment), but viewed from different perspectives. Saint Paul tells us that all of creation groans as it waits for its redemption (Rom 8:22), and John the Revelator shows us what that ultimate redemption will look like (Rev 21), while shamanism shows us just how involved all of creation actually is in that redemption. Studying the one can—without doubt in my mind, anyway—endlessly enrich the practice of the other.

Daniel: John, you've given us a wonderful "big picture"

perspective. However, shamanism, like Christianity, recognizes that there is plenty of room and need for healing in our present ordinary world—not every being here is presently contributing toward the healing and wholeness that is unfolding and is our hope for the future.

Christianity gives us the gift of Jesus as the "fully human and fully divine" picture of what God is up to in this world. Christians see Jesus's death and resurrection as the powerful sign of God's overcoming sin and death and bringing forgiveness, reconciliation, healing, and wholeness to humanity. Christianity emphasizes action in, by, and through community. We are not just individuals alone, we belong beyond ourselves and are together empowered by the Holy Spirit working in our midst to bring Christ's love to the world. There is a strong social gospel tradition that links work to overcome human suffering and oppression with community action and involvement in movements for justice and liberation. Christianity has a mystical tradition that can be applied in our prayer and meditation for direct spiritual encounter with the Divine and for healing and guidance in our daily living.

Shamanism, an ancient tradition predating any of our world religions, taps into our human capacity for spiritual wonder and provides tools for entering into the spiritual dimensions of reality. Shamanism opens up the cosmos and brings us into contact with the worlds of spirits. Here we can build alliances, even friendships, with powerful and compassionate spirits that help us and those we serve move toward that wholeness for which we all long. Shamanism awakens us to the aliveness of all creation. It sensitizes us in a whole new way to the beauty of the Earth and bids us be contributing members of the whole; in respectful relationship, kinship, to other species and forms of life.

7

CONCLUSION

DANIEL L. PRECHTEL

Expanding our Vision
of Divine Grace and Community

"Have you understood all this?" They answered, "Yes." And Jesus said to them, "Therefore every scribe who has been trained for the kingdom of heaven is like the master of a household who brings out of his treasure what is new and what is old."
    —*Matthew 13:51-52*

Shamanism, including shamanic ascension, is a path of independence leading toward spiritual freedom. By spiritual freedom, I mean freedom to know, not just to believe... We no longer are restricted to the teachings of the Heavenly Books brought to us by the ancient few, for now the many can travel to the sacred origins of the teachings themselves. Like a spiritual Liberty Bell, the shaman's drum declares the start of a spiritual revolution, however long it may take. The severed vine to the heavens has been restored. Also restored is the way below, down the metaphoric roots of the vine to realms long denied.

—Michael Harner[1]

*W*e have explored rich treasures that can equip us for encounters with the spiritual realm to the benefit of humanity and a transformed relationship with the earth and its myriad life forms. Some shamanic methods may be tens of millennia old, carried forward by countless generations of seers, wisdom keepers, and healers. Most Western Europeans and Anglo-Americans lost much of this ancient shamanic tradition through centuries of domination by the collusion between militant Christian and sociopolitical governing powers. With the rise of the age of Enlightenment, much of what remained from mystical spiritual traditions and shamanic cultures was suppressed, or at least viewed with suspicion as being superstitious and irrational. However, some indigenous shamanic cultures survived; and in Christianity the treasures of mystical prayer and spiritual healing were preserved and carried forward in some branches of the faith.

Several movements rising in the past forty to sixty years have brought us to a very special opportunity in spiritual development. One movement that affects us as a species (and many other species) is the growing awareness of how humans are critically damaging our global environment—the ecological movement and the growth of ecospirituality. Our dominant culture lacked the spiritual values for sustaining a respectful relationship with the Earth and its species, values that have been carried through millennia in indigenous cultures. In the past, the Christian religion has often failed to give emphasis to the goodness of God's creation and our human role of caring for it, and instead saw creation as something over which humans were divinely commissioned to dominate. That latter view gave a false moral consent to economic interests to exploit the earth for immediate gain without consideration for sustainability and mutuality. But criticism of such a theology of greed and exploitation is gaining a strong and prevailing voice within the Church. This is God's world and all of creation belongs to the Creator. We are a part of the creation and called to take a responsible and respectful role in it.

Core shamanism, learning from the deep wisdom of indigenous shamanic cultures, provides tools for our deepened sensitivity to Earth and its myriad forms of life. We are not set apart from creation, but are interrelated in a kinship network of all life. Our journeys to learn from power animal spirits, or from the spirits of nature in the Middle World, or from wise and compassionate Upper or Lower World teachers deepen our connection and interrelatedness to the web of life. Our journeys take us along paths of healing and wholeness that include human beings in creative partnerships with other beings.

Another movement has arisen within the Christian Church, but is also reflected in our general society. Since the 1960s there has been a great interest in experiential methods for enhancing spiritual awareness and engaging in mystical practices. People are less interested in knowing *about* God than in directly knowing God, building a relationship with the Divine, and having personal experience of the sacred in living. Spiritual guidance as a ministry offered to the general population has been on the increase for fifty years and many institutes and certificate training programs make formation available in particular spiritual traditions, Christian ecumenical programs, and in recent years, some interfaith settings. People have also been seeking the Divine outside of the Christian religion, hungry for spiritual experience through teachers from other great faith traditions, and in nonreligious settings. Training with indigenous shamans and medicine men and women, or in cross-culturally-based shamanic training programs, has been increasingly available over the past forty years.

Alongside these movements have come the ecumenical movement within Christianity and a corresponding movement to build interfaith relationships between major religious traditions. These movements have been exploring what we hold in common as well as how to relate to the places of difference with greater respect. High walls of distrust, vicious rivalry, and ignorance were built over centuries between Christian denominations and between major faith traditions. But those walls are slowly being dismantled and new creative relationships are being constructed within an atmosphere of respect and appreciation. Even though we still have a long way to go, we are realizing that we have much that we can learn from each other.

These movements are actually happening relatively fast in terms of human history. The rapid growth in global communication certainly is a factor. The pressure to make serious healthy changes in response to global challenges and crises is also a significant influence. We have to face the possibility of our nuclear technology bringing on global disaster, or the likelihood of severe consequences due to unchecked climate change. But these severe challenges are a call to humanity to step into new spiritual maturity. It seems to me that we are being assisted in this by *God's intention and power.*

Do you not hear it? Do you not feel the pull? From beyond ourselves, and yet consonant with our deepest inner wisdom, is an invitation both ancient and immediately urgent and fresh. Sacred Mystery, intuited throughout human history—variously clothed and named by countless cultures—still tugs at us and invites us to make journeys of discovery into the realms of spirit to bring back to our ordinary reality gifts of compassion and knowledge.

Various traditions have commemorated and revered those

who have made such journeys in the past. Some have been founders of religions and their teachings have been enshrined for the edification of future generations. And certainly there is much we can receive and give from those religions and their practices. But Michael Harner taught that the journeys to the spirit realms need not be restricted to just a few specially chosen individuals and that the sources of divine revelation and what societies would call miracles are not closed to contemporary journeyers. Core shamanism welcomes those who are adherents of religious traditions, as well as those who do not profess a religious faith, but emphasizes the direct, personal experience gained by shamanic journeying rather than relying on a system of beliefs that are derived from others' experiences.

How does this apply in the case of the Christian religion? Within the Christian tradition there are both doctrines—teachings developed and passed on in the Church that provide an orientation to covenantal relationships with God, other people, and creation—and spiritual practices that help us experientially develop those relationships. The doctrines comprise a system of collective beliefs rooted in the ancient sacred stories and revelations of God's work with humans and creation. But certain forms of prayer and meditation, such as the practices we have discussed in this book, help us directly engage the divine Presence and aligned spiritual beings that are part of nonordinary reality. Some of these spiritual practices are personal and individually applied, but there is always a communal context as well, because Christianity is communal by nature and set in a dynamic relationship with the Triune God.

Christian sacred scriptures point to Jesus' life: his teachings, healing ministry and "miraculous" events, and the powerful significance of his manner of death, resurrection, and ascension. Jesus proclaimed to the common people the nearness of the "kingdom of God" and saw that his life would be like a grain of wheat that falls to the earth and dies and bears much fruit (John 12:24), and that his followers would do greater works than his (John 14:12). That divine power and presence of the crucified and resurrected Jesus was spread by the Holy Spirit to Jesus' followers and made them part of a "new creation."

We have maintained that Christian spiritual orientations and practices can be compatible with core shamanism. Even more, we see that these two spiritual orientations (shamanic and Christian) with their journey and prayer methods are mutually enriching while also challenging the practitioner. We do not wish to "convert" either the Christian or the Core Shamanic practitioner, but rather to introduce these spiritual traditions to each other and recognize the gifts both have for our common humanity and its relationships, both for ordinary and nonordinary realities. We hope that our introductions to Core Shamanism and the visionary in Christian experience, our personal stories, our conversation with readers, and the integrity of our different perspectives have helped do this for you.

For Christians in this present time: our religion has much to repent of in its institutional misuse of power and authority and its theological arrogance and exclusivism. Is the Holy One leading us to look beyond our closed tribal identity and our narrow doctrines to share in a greater reality, and embrace a greater "communion of saints" than we have previously envisioned? I remember when I first went to a weekend training through the Foundation for Shamanic Studies. After all my hesitation and worry about how, as an ordained Christian minister, I would be received (by both the shamanic and Christian communities) once I was with the people at the workshop I suddenly felt like they, too, were my people and part of my expanding spiritual family. I belonged with them, too. We can best know whether this is God's desire for us if we test it out through our own direct experience. It takes a lot of courage to explore this because the boundaries have been drawn very narrowly for centuries with lots of suspicion about the "others." But this is *our* time when we are invited by the Spirit to look both at the old treasures and new ones emerging for the purposes of participating in God's expanding realm "on earth as it is in heaven."

For shamanic practitioners: I am acutely sensitive to the fact that various forms of Christianity have done much damage throughout our history, and there are many people today who have been excluded, injured, or severely restricted by a use of institutional power and authority that does not reflect the central gospel message of God's unconditional love or Jesus' path of peace and reconciliation. But there were and there are many faithful Christians who embrace the values of Jesus and live in the power and loving ways of the Spirit. Can you be open to a Christianity that is spiritually hospitable and inclusive? Can you look for Christians that are different than the militant and exclusive varieties that claim themselves as the religion's true and sole representatives? For we are here and offer our friendship.

Think of a beautiful large orchard where there are many varieties of trees producing succulent fruit of different kinds for nurture and healing. Our various spiritual traditions and faiths, all rooted in the fertile soil of deep Mystery, belong together as relatives in mutual service to our common humanity and the greater creation of which we are a part.

An invitation is given to us, from beyond ourselves, to expand our vision and the practices that engage spiritual reality. That expansive vision shifts us to a deep respect for each spiritual tradition's gifts for the common good. It encourages us to see ourselves as belonging to a deeper and broader kinship network than previously understood; not only of humans, but of the whole of creation—both that which we can ordinarily see and that which is beyond our usual perceptions. It calls us to greater compassion for each other, and profound respect and gratitude for the One who holds us all in unfathomable love and kindness.

GLOSSARY

Animism | The view that everything is alive and has a spirit.

Apocalyptic | Revelations about the inner workings of the cosmos or the ultimate destiny of the world.

Apocryphal | Early Jewish and Christian writings not always carrying canonical authority.

Ascension (of Jesus) | Forty days after his resurrection, Jesus went to dwell in heaven with God. Jesus no longer limited to ordinary space and time.

Christian Fundamentalism | Teaching that everything in the Bible is to be literally interpreted and that everything points to Jesus Christ's lordship.

Communion of the Saints | The belief that through Christ the living and dead are held in communion by God's love.

Core Shamanism | A contemporary school of shamanism featuring methods and understandings derived from universal, near-universal, and common practices of indigenous shamanic cultures.

Deities | Gods and goddesses.

Deliverance | Religious practices for freeing people from invasive spirit attachment, influence, oppression, and possession.

Depossession | Shamanic method for releasing spirits from attaching, influencing, oppressing, or possessing a person.

Discernment | Spiritual practice for perceiving forces at work in issues; seeking divine wisdom and guidance.

Divination | In shamanism, seeking guidance and knowledge from a helping spirit.

Eschatological | Pertaining to the ultimate or last things.

Eucharist | A Christian sacramental rite that makes Christians present at Jesus' Last Supper (in the past) and, simultaneously, at the great feast at the end of time (in the future). Christians believe that Jesus' presence is mystically received in the consecrated bread and wine.

Holy Trinity | The Christian belief in the unity of the three persons of God.

Imaginal | Pertaining to a realm of reality accessed by the power of imagination.

Interspiritual | The spiritual perspective that views all faith traditions as emerging from one source, converging in a mystical core of authentic spirituality and manifested in shared teachings and values.

Interworld Zones | In shamanism, regions in the Middle World where discarnate human souls dwell that have not yet moved to the Upper or Lower Worlds.

Intrusive Spirit | A low level spirit that invades a human or other being.

Liturgical | Pertaining to corporate worship; can refer to rites or texts detailing those rites.

Lower World | In shamanism, a nonordinary world of nature where discarnate spirits (often plant and animal) live and grow.

Jungian | A school of psychoanalysis derived from the work of Carl G. Jung, including his teaching on the power of archetypes.

Metaphysical | Without physical form or substance, but spiritually based.

Middle World | In shamanism, the world of physicality,

commonly agreed on as real, but which also has a nonordinary spirit dimension.

Monotheistic | A religious belief in one God.

Mythic | Storied, legendary, derived from myth.

Noetic | Relating to the mind or intellect.

Nonordinary Reality | A dimension or realm of existence where spirits are encountered; the Otherworld.

Ontologically | Related to the nature of being.

Otherworld | The realms of nonordinary reality.

Psychopomp | A conductor helping discarnate souls move to their next world.

Pseudepigraphal | Related to non-canonical Jewish or Christian religious texts from two hundred years before and after the common era.

Post-Constantinian | Institutional Christian religion empowered by the Roman Empire of Constantine the Great and his successors.

Power Animal | A guardian animal spirit from the Lower World.

Purgatory | In some Christian spiritual cosmologies, a region of afterlife intended for the purification of souls.

Reductionism | Reducing complex processes or phenomena to simple, often material, and mechanistic terms.

Resurrection | In Christianity, the Easter event of Jesus being raised by God from death to new life that becomes the hope for humanity.

Shaman | One who journeys to nonordinary reality to make alliances with spirits that help with knowledge and healing.

Shamanic Journey | The intentional journey into nonordinary reality to interact with spirits.

Shamanic State of Consciousness | A trance state that allows for journeys into nonordinary reality.

Soul | The enduring spirit of a being that is part of the natural world (not a human creation).

Spirit | The essence of any being.

Spiritual Director | A guide for supporting a person's spiritual life.

Teacher (Spirit) | A highly evolved, compassionate tutelary spirit usually from the Upper or Lower World.

Transfiguration (of Jesus) | A biblical event where Jesus, clothed in brilliant whiteness, is seen by three of his disciples conversing with Moses and Elijah.

Triumphalist | The assertion of a victorious and superior status or creed by some Christians.

Upper World | In shamanism, a celestial nonordinary world where discarnate spirits dwell and thrive.

Vision/Visionary | Perceiving nonordinary reality by a dream or a waking state of altered consciousness.

APPENDIX 1

DANIEL L. PRECHTEL

Apophatic and Kataphatic Sides of Christian and Core Shamanic Spiritual Experience

In Christian spiritual experience there are two major dimensions pertinent to our exploration of shamanism and Christian prayer and meditation. The negative way or apophatic side of spiritual experience emphasizes the mystery of the Divine. God, from this perspective, can never be fully grasped and is beyond all of our images and understanding. Spiritual practices associated with this side of spiritual experience include centering prayer, silence, and self-emptying. We may receive an intuition of God's presence as we yearn for union with the One, but the focus is on the God beyond our senses and knowledge. The stripping away of images, while helpful as a profound intuitive way of simply being present to, with, and in the Divine, does not accommodate well to shamanic exploration of nonordinary reality and activity in partnership with spirits—even if they are agents of Divine grace. On the other hand, the apophatic way does safeguard against the human tendency to make idols of the various powers that impact our lives. This way insists that there is only one God that is the source of our being and worthy of our worship.

The affirmative way, or kataphatic side of spiritual experience emphasizes that God is knowable and accessible. Christians readily point to Jesus as the full human incarnation of God. If we want to know what God is like and what God desires for humankind we can look to the stories and visualizations of Jesus. We also get glimpses of God's grandeur, creativity, and presence in and through nature and beauty, worship and scripture, and in numerous other ways. Prayer and meditation practices that use our capacity to visualize or otherwise sense the presence of the Divine, or the agents of divinity, are very close to shamanic journey experience. Our visions and dreams become subject matter for revealing elements of nonordinary reality and the wisdom and healing that can come as gifts from "beyond" us. However, in order for the Divine to be sensible to us, we typically need to experience divinity in representational forms. We experience the Holy One in and through things and people. In the Christian kataphatic way, God, and God's grace (power), comes to us not only as the Holy Trinity, but by countless means, including images, metaphors, symbols, sacraments, and icons. So too, the shamanic practitioner meets and works in alliance with Upper and Lower World spirits that manifest the compassion, wisdom, maturity, and healing ability that would be evidence of the working of the Spirit.

I have found that these apophatic and kataphatic sides to spiritual life have a kind of fluidity and are not rigid polarities or mutually exclusive of one-another. They are both hard-wired into our human nature as capacities for experiencing the wonder and mystery of the Divine. As a Christian and a shamanic practitioner I encounter those dimensions in my own spiritual journey explorations. I can "see" and interact with saints, wise teachers, Jesus, angels, and marvelous animal spirits. Those encounters come from the kataphatic dimension of spiritual experience. But I also experience a sense of the hiddenness of God in that nothing in my visions can express the fullness of Divinity.

I've had a few situations where I glimpsed a little of God's majesty and power. In one dream when I sought the presence of God I was immediately blinded, but then led to a garden by a powerful but gentle hand grasping my heart. In another dream I entered "The Diamond Room," where I had a fleeting view of a huge living jewel that radiated amazing colors around the room. I was in the presence of two magnificent angelic guardians. The brief sight brought me to my knees in wonder and awe and then I awoke. And in a shamanic journey to an angelic realm I was given the opportunity to visit the "angelic council." It looked like a galaxy filled with moving stars (angels) that formed concentric circles around a center that was a massive, luminous living sphere of energy and intelligence. All of these visionary experiences not only had a strong kataphatic element, but they also conveyed the apophatic intuition that these are very limited representations of the One who is unlimited and cannot be contained. They were all incredibly moving experiences, while also leaving me humbled and in wonder.

In the literature about Core Shamanism it is emphasized that this is not a belief system, but rather a gathering of methods and teaching from across indigenous shamanic cultures to give practitioners with a Western orientation the practical tools necessary to directly engage spirits and journey into nonordinary spiritual reality. It is available to anyone interested in making experiential journeys, to those who hold to particular religious teachings and those who do not. Patterns do emerge in the collective experiences of the practitioners that show the general contours of spiritual cosmology and how we can interact with spirits. However, there is no claim that God (or various gods) oversees and compassionately influences the spiritual realms. Many practitioners have the sense that this is the situation, and my own Christian orientation gives me a framework for understanding what is going on in this way. But many other practitioners worthy of respect will come to different understandings or will be content to let such big questions remain mysteries. Ultimately, the shamanic path, at least through Core Shamanism, invites practitioners into wondrous kataphatic experiences, but also holds the vastness of these realms in an apophatic mystery that transcends any claim to the supremacy of a particular religious understanding.

APPENDIX 2

DANIEL L. PRECHTEL

A Visit to the Wise One

Wisdom has built her house,
she has hewn her seven pillars,
She has slaughtered her animals,
she has mixed her wine,
she has also set her table.
She has sent out her servant girls,
she calls from the highest places in town,
"You that are simple, turn in here!"
To those without sense she says,
"Come, eat of my bread
and drink of the wine I have mixed.
Lay aside immaturity, and live
and walk in the way of insight."
—Proverbs 9:1-6

- Close your eyes, take a few slow deep breaths, and ask the Spirit to take you to a special place in spiritual reality where you can do this work.

- Look around and notice what you see and feel. Immerse yourself in this place and open your senses to being present there.
- You may call in helpers to accompany you to the Wise One.
- Begin your journey to the house where the Wise One dwells.
- As you approach the Wise One's house, take a moment to notice what the place looks like and how you feel about being there.
- When you reach the door to the house of the Wise One, knock at the door and enter when you are bidden to do so.
- Look around the room and look at the Wise One. What do you see in the room? How does the Wise One appear to you? How do you feel about being in the Wise One's presence?
- You may have a question for the Wise One or you might wish to tell the Wise One about something that you are now considering. Ask the Wise One's counsel on whatever you wish, and listen for his or her reply. If you need further clarification, feel free to engage in further conversation with the Wise One.
- The Wise One may offer something special for you. It might be a special word or phrase for you to take with you, or an object, or a song, or some other gift. If offered, receive whatever gift the Wise One has for you, and feel free to ask about it if you need to know more. Respond to the Wise One's giving in whatever way you think is appropriate.
- It is now time to make your farewell to the Wise One. Do so, and then begin your journey back, remembering your time with the Wise One and

whatever you received from your visit, knowing also that you can visit the Wise One again…and whenever you are ready, open your eyes and bring your attention fully back to ordinary reality and your place in it.

APPENDIX 3

DANIEL L. PRECHTEL

A Visit to the Healer

- Close your eyes, take a few slow deep breaths, and ask the Spirit to take you to a special place in spiritual reality where you can do this work.
- Look around and notice what you see and feel. Immerse yourself in this place and open your senses to being present there.
- You may call in helpers to accompany you to the Healer.
- Begin your journey to the house where the Healer dwells.
- As you approach the Healer's house take a moment to notice what the place looks like and how you feel about being there.
- When you reach the door to the house of the Healer, knock at the door and enter when you are invited to do so.
- Look around the room and look at the Healer. What

do you see in the room? Who or what does the Healer look like to you? Are there others in the room?

- You may bring your concern or healing need for yourself or for someone else to the Healer. Tell or show the Healer whatever your need is and answer any questions the Healer may have for you. Ask any questions you might have for the Healer and listen for the Healer's reply.

- If you are coming to the Healer with someone else who has given you permission to do this spiritual healing work on their behalf, bring that person to the Healer and let them engage each other. Simply stand with your friend, perhaps with a hand on his/her shoulder.

- Let the Healer give you (or the person you brought) whatever healing actions are offered. It might be a healing touch, light that radiates healing, a special word or phrase, or an object that is given or removed, or some other representation addressing your healing need. The Healer may also seal you in some way with protection.

- The Healer may also have a special gift for you. If so, receive the gift the Healer has for you, and feel free to ask about it if you need to know more. Respond to the Healer's gift in whatever way you think is appropriate.

- It is now time to make your farewell to the Healer. Do so, and then begin your journey back...remembering your time with the Healer and whatever you received from your visit, knowing also that you can visit the Healer again...and whenever you are ready, open your eyes and bring your attention fully back to ordinary reality and your place in it.

APPENDIX 4

DANIEL L. PRECHTEL

Making Shamanic Journeys to the Lower and Upper World

The Lower and Upper World are very important locations in shamanism since they are the regions where compassionate, highly evolved, and powerful spirits reside. So a shamanic practitioner will want to learn how to get to those worlds and enter into relationship with the spirits there. Traditionally the way to journey to those worlds is by entering into a shamanic state of consciousness, usually with the aid of a drumbeat or rattle at four to seven beats per second. The practitioner sets an intention in the shamanic trance to look for a way to travel either in the lower or upper direction. A tree can be a good vehicle for this travel. One can enter the tree and follow the roots down to the Lower World or travel up through the center of the tree to the Upper World. Often it will look like moving through a tunnel going in the direction the practitioner wishes to journey. Other means of journeying include entering a lake and diving down to its depths and entering the Lower World, or following the rising smoke of a fire to the Upper World. Some practitioners will enter a cave or a hole in the ground and go down a tunnel, or climb a mountain and go beyond the clouds. These are just a few examples of envisioned ways of journeying beyond the Middle World and entering the Lower or Upper World.

Since the Middle World's nonordinary reality has many levels, it is possible to think you have journeyed beyond that world but may not actually have done so. To be assured of leaving the Middle World, the shamanic practitioner may often encounter a barrier or membrane that must be passed through in order to enter the other worlds. Perhaps on the journey down you encounter a wall or dense cluster of roots that seem to block your passage. Since this is a spirit journey, you can easily pass through the barrier and enter the Lower World. Or you may find a layer of cloud or mist to pass beyond that symbolizes the threshold to the Upper World. These worlds also have many levels to them and travel between the levels is similar to your initial journey. Exploring the Lower and Upper World is in itself a fascinating and informative adventure, but the primary objective of the shamanic practitioner is to make allies of some of the spirits of these worlds.

Usually the first shamanic journey is made to the Lower World with the intention of seeking a power animal as an ally. Upon entering the Lower World, look around and see if there is an animal (mammal, bird, reptile, or amphibian) that is near you or coming toward you. Be open to what animal is there for you —for it may not be what you anticipated. If there is an animal close by ask it if it is your power animal. The animal will respond to your question positively or negatively: by speaking, nodding, or giving you some other sign. If it is not meant to be your power animal it may walk or fly away or simply ignore you. If it bares its teeth or fangs in a threatening manner you are not meant to be in relationship with it and you simply move away from it. If it is meant to be your power animal take what- ever time you have remaining in your journey to begin to know your power animal. You can ask questions about its attributes and powers, how it can aid you, what it would like to do with you. Ask if it would like to show you something or teach you something. In subsequent visits you will build a deeper relationship with this animal.

If you feel that you do not wish to be in a relationship with that particular animal spirit, you are free to look for a different power animal. The animal you do not choose will not be offended—it is not self-centered.

Sometimes you will not find a power animal in your immediate vicinity. In that case you can explore the area and see if you come upon an animal or a variety of animals. Call out, asking for help, shouting that you are looking for your power animal. If no power animal becomes apparent on this journey, do not lose hope. You may need to make further journeys. Sometimes a power animal will test you to be sure you are capable of taking the relationship seriously. It is well worth the effort! A power animal can be an important protector in the Middle World. Some can help guide you to destinations in any of the worlds, the animal may assist you in divination questions, and some offer healing assistance. You may have more than one power animal, and some may be given to you through the work of another practitioner doing a spirit retrieval journey on your behalf.

Once you have a power animal as a helping spirit, you may decide to journey to the Upper World in search of a teacher. You might ask your power animal if it will help you find a teacher in the Upper World, or you may make the journey on your own. When you arrive in the Upper World you will look for spirits there that are potentially your teacher. Often these spirits will have the appearance of being human, angelic, or a deity. Remember that these spirits are compassionate, wise, and safe to be with. When you come up to such a spirit simply ask if it is your teacher. The spirit might answer in the positive, or redirect you, or may simply ignore you. Keep asking various spirits until you come across your teacher, or receive a positive response to your call for your teacher to come to you. Once you encounter your teacher (tutelary spirit) spend the bulk of your time getting acquainted. You might ask for a teaching, or ask for healing. A teacher is someone you can receive wise guidance and healing from, and learn from about other spirits and the worlds you interact in. They can teach you how to be more effective as a shamanic practitioner. Sometimes a teacher might give you something that will assist you in particular circumstances. Like with power animals, teachers may accompany you in your journeys to the nonordinary reality of the Middle World.

NOTES

INTRODUCTION

1. We will explain this term in detail later, but in brief, Core Shamanism is a system of practice culled from those elements common to most shamanic traditions.

1. SHAMANIC JOURNEYS TO THE WORLDS OF SPIRITS

1. Harner, *Cave and Cosmos*, 40-45.
2. For a fuller discussion of ethics see the article by Susan Mokelke, https://www.shamanism.org/articles/ethics.html.
3. Harner, *Cave and Cosmos*, 99.
4. Rowden, *Christianity and Nature-based Spirituality*, 28.

2. THE VISIONARY & SHAMANISTIC IN CHRISTIANITY

1. Henry Corbin, "Mundus Imaginalis or The Imaginary and the Imaginal," *Spring Journal* (1972): 4.
2. *Hamlet* (1.5.167-8)
3. Corbin, p. 5.
4. Daniel writes more about this, but I'll include the broad outlines here as a means of comparison.
5. Corbin, p. 15.
6. U2 borrowed this quote for their song, "Walk On," which is where I first heard it.
7. *Flowing Light of the Godhead*, p. 102.
8. It is also the first book we possess written by a woman in English.
9. The term "active imagination" was invented by C.G. Jung.
10. Newman, John Henry. "Holiness Necessary for Future Blessedness," from *Parochial and Plain Sermons*. London: Longmans, Green; 1834.
11. From *Purgatory*, by Fr. F. X. Schouppe, SJ (London: Burns, Oates & Washbourne, Ltd, 1893), pps. 16–19.
12. Swedenborg, *Worlds in Space* (1758), 93.
13. No doubt influenced by Colossians 1:16, "For by him were all things

created, that are in heaven, and that are in earth, visible and invisible, whether they be thrones, or dominions, or principalities, or powers."
14. Ignatius of Antioch, Epistle to the Ephesians.
15. Sermon on the Sinful Woman.

4. MY SHAMANIC EXPERIENCES

1. Regina Baümer and Michael Plattig, "Desert Fathers and Spiritual Direction," in *Presence*, Summer 2001.
2. Charles Williams, *The Greater Trumps* (London: Victor Gollancz, 1932), p. 219.
3. For more on the practice of exchange in the Christian tradition, please see my article, "The Practice of Exchange in Spiritual Direction," published in *Presence*, Vol. 19.1.

5. HEALING, KNOWLEDGE & GUIDANCE

1. *An Invocation for Divine Help* was developed from a shamanic journey where the spirit of Jesus gave me the chant tune. Further meditation with Jesus gave me the words to this "power song." You can hear me sing the chant at https://www.youtube.com/watch?v=a1Lm604Cn0o.
2. Prologue, *Rule of St. Benedict.*
3. Rev. Bobbie McKay, Ph.D. and Lewis A. Musil, *Healing the Spirit: Stories of Transformation* (Allen, TX: ThomasMore, 2000), 65. Stories in Chapters 8-10 are organized around the kinds of spiritual healing.
4. A template for the visit to Wisdom meditation is included as Appendix 2.
5. A template for the visit to the Healer meditation is included as Appendix 3.
6. I strongly commend reading Pieter F. Craffert, *The Life of a Galilean Shaman: Jesus of Nazareth in Anthropological-Historical Perspective*, Matrix: The Bible in Mediterranean Context, Volume 3, (Eugene, OR: Cascade Books, Wipf and Stock Publishers, 2008). Craffert presents a fascinating discussion of healing paradigms in Chapter 9: "Healing, Exorcism and Control of Spirits."

6. GOING DEEPER

1. See John's discussion of the "imaginal" in chapter 2.
2. Harner, *Cave and Cosmos*, 137.
3. For more on this idea, see Scott McKnight, *A Theology Called Atonement* (Nashville, TN: Abingdon, 2007).
4. Bly, *The Kabir Book*, #19, 24-25.

7. CONCLUSION

1. Harner, *Cave and Cosmos*, 216.

BIBLIOGRAPHY

Allen, Sue. *Spirit Release: A Practical Handbook.* Winchester, UK: O Books, 2007.

Arrien, Angeles. *The Four-Fold Way: Walking the Paths of the Warrior, Teacher, Healer, and Visionary.* NY: HarperOne, 1993.

Baldwin, William J. *Spirit Releasement: A Technique Manual.* Second edition. Terra Alta, WV: 1992.

Bly, Robert. *The Kabir Book: Forty-Four of the Ecstatic Poems of Kabir.* Versions by Robert Bly. A Seventies Press Book. Boston: Beacon Press. 1977.

Bohler, Carolyn Stahl. *Opening to God: Guided Imagery Meditation on Scripture.* Revised and expanded edition. Nashville: Upper Room Books, 1996.

Brooke, Avery. *Healing in the Landscape of Prayer.* Boston: Cowley Publications, 1996.

Cheetham, Tom. *All the World an Icon: Henry Corbin and the Angelic Function of Beings.* Berkeley: North Atlantic Books, 2012.

Cowan, Tom. *Fire in the Head: Shamanism and the Celtic Spirit.* New York: HarperOne, 1993.
—. *Shamanism: As a Spiritual Practice for Daily Life.* Berkeley: Crossing Press, 1996.
—. *Yearning for the Wind: Celtic Reflections on Nature and the Soul.* Forward by Sandra Ingerman. Novato, CA: New World Library, 2003.

Craffert, Pieter F. *The Life of a Galilean Shaman: Jesus of Nazareth in Anthropological-Historical Perspective.* MATRIX: The Bible in Mediterranean Context series. Eugene, OR: Cascade Books, 2008.

Eliade, Mircea. *Shamanism: Archaic Techniques of Ecstasy.* Bollingen Series 76. Princeton: Princeton University Press, 1964. Second paperback edition with a new forward by Wendy Doniger, 2004.

Glass-Coffin, Bonnie and don Oscar Miro-Quesada. *Lessons in Courage: Peruvian Shamanic Wisdom for Everyday Life.* Faber, VA: Rainbow Ridge Books, 2013.

Greer, Carl. *Change Your Story, Change Your Life: Using Shamanic and Jungian Tools to Achieve Personal Transformation.* Forward by Alberto Villoldo. Scotland, UK: Findhorn Press, 2014.
—. *Change the Story of Your Health: Using Shamanic and Jungian Techniques for Healing.* Forward by Melinda Ring. Scotland, UK: 2017.

Harner, Michael. *Cave and Cosmos: Shamanic Encounters with Another Reality.* Berkeley: North Atlantic Books, 2013.

—. *The Way of the Shaman.* New York: HarperOne, 1980, 1990.

Harrell, Mary. *Imaginal Figures in Everyday Life: Stories from the World Between Matter and Mind.* Forward by Robert Romanyshyn. Ashville: Chiron/InnerQuest Books, 2015. (Jungian "Imaginal" psychoanalytic approach.)

Ingerman, Sandra. *Medicine for the Earth: How to Transform Personal and Environmental Toxins.* New York: Three Rivers Press, 2000.
—. *Soul Retrieval: Mending the Fragmented Self.* Forward by Michael Harner. New York: HarperSanFrancisco, 1991.

Ingerman, Sandra and Hank Wesselman. *Awakening to the Spirit World: The Shamanic Path of Direct Revelation.* Boulder: Sounds True, 2010.

Ingerman, Sandra and Llyn Roberts. *Speaking with Nature: Awakening to the Deep Wisdom of the Earth.* Rochester, VT: Bear & Company, 2015.

Ireland-Frey, Louise. *Freeing the Captives: The Emerging Therapy of Treating Spirit Attachment.* Charlottesville, VA: Hampton Roads, 1999.

Kalsched, Donald. *Trauma and the Soul: A Psycho-spiritual Approach to Human Development and its Interruption.* New York: Routledge, 2013. (Jungian analytic therapy.)

Keeney, Bradford. *Shamanic Christianity: The Direct Experience of Mystical Communion.* Rochester, VT: Destiny Books, 2006.

Kelsey, Morton. *Companions on the Inner Way: The Art of Spiritual Guidance.* New York: Crossroad Publishing, 1996.

—. *Healing and Christianity: A Classic Study.* Minneapolis: Augsburg Fortress, 1995.

—. *Transcend: A Guide to the Spiritual Quest.* New York: Crossroad Publishing, 1981.

Lame Deer, John (Fire) and Richard Erdoes. *Lame Deer: Seeker of Visions.* New York, Pocket Books, 1976.

Linn, Dennis and Matthew. *Healing of Memories: Prayer and Confession—Steps to Inner Healing.* New York: Paulist Press, 1974.

MacNutt, Francis. *Deliverance from Evil Spirits: A Practical Manual.* Grand Rapids: Chosen Books, 1995.

McKay, Bobbie and Lewis A Musil. *Healing the Spirit: Stories of Transformation.* Forward by John Shea. Allen, TX: Thomas More Publishing, 2000.

McKnight, Scott. *A Theology Called Atonement.* Nashville, TN: Abingdon, 2007.

Moss, Nan and David Corbin. *Weather Shamanism: Harmonizing our Connection with the Elements.* Rochester, VT: Bear & Company, 2008.

Moss, Robert. *Conscious Dreaming: A Spiritual Path for Everyday Life.* New York: Three Rivers Press, 1996.

Neihardt, John G. *Black Elk Speaks: Being the Life Story of a Holy Man of the Oglala Sioux.* New York: Pocket Books, 1973.

Perry, Michael, ed. *Deliverance: Psychic Disturbances and Occult Involvement.* Second edition from the Christian Deliverance

Study Group. London: SPCK, 1996. (Basis for training of diocesan deliverance teams in the Church of England.)

Prechtel, Daniel L. *Light on the Path: Guiding Symbols for Insight and Discernment: Meeting God through Dreams, Sacraments, Stories, Meditation, and Spiritual Practice.* New York: Morehouse Publishing, 2016.

Prechtel, Martín. *Secrets of the Talking Jaguar: Memoirs from the Living Heart of a Mayan Village.* Forward by Robert Bly. New York: Tarcher/Penguin, 1998.

Rowden, Lillie. *Christianity and Nature-based Spirituality: A Shamanic Journey through the Medicine Wheel.* Wimberley, TX: 2nd Tier Publishing, 2014.

Salomone, Peter. *Shamanic Depossession: A Compassionate Healing Practice.* Placerville, CA: Visione Sciamanica, 2014.

Sanford, Agnes. *The Healing Light.* Thirteenth edition. First published in 1947. St. Paul, MN: Macalester Park Publishing, 1968. (Classic in the Christian spiritual healing movement.)

Some, Malidoma Patrice. *Of Water and the Spirit: Ritual, Magic, and Initiation in the Life of an African Shaman.* NY: Penguin Books, 1994.

Stolzman, William. *The Pipe and Christ: A Christian-Sioux Dialogue.* Sixth edition. Chamberlain, SD: Tipi Press, 1998.

Underhill, Ruth Murray. *Singing for Power: The Song Magic of the Papago Indians of Southern Arizona.* New York: Ballantine, 1938. Reprinted 1968.

Villoldo, Alberto. *The Heart of the Shaman: Stories and Practices of the Luminous Warrior*. Carlsbad, CA: Hay House, 2018.

Waddell, Helen. *Beasts and Saints*. Introduced and edited by Esther de Waal. First published in 1934. Grand Rapids: William B. Eerdmans Publishing, 1995.

Wink, Walter. *Naming the Powers: The Language of Power in the New Testament*. Volume One of the Powers Trilogy. Philadelphia: Fortress Press, 1984.
—. *Unmasking the Powers: The Invisible Forces that Determine Human Existence*. Volume Two of the Powers Trilogy. Philadelphia: Fortress Press, 1986.
—. *Engaging the Powers: Discernment and Resistance in a World of Domination*. Volume Three of the Powers Trilogy. Minneapolis: Fortress Press, 1992.

Williams, Charles. *The Greater Trumps*. London: Victor Gollancz, 1932.

Wuellner, Flora Slosson. *Prayer and Our Bodies*. Nashville: The Upper Room, 1987.
—. *Prayer, Stress, and Our Inner Wounds*. Nashville: The Upper Room, 1985.

ABOUT THE AUTHORS

DANIEL L. PRECHTEL

Rev. Daniel Prechtel is an ordained priest of the Episcopal Church since 1984 and operates Lamb & Lion Spiritual Guidance Ministries since 1993. He holds a master of divinity degree and a doctor of ministry degree. He is a priest assisting at All Souls Episcopal Parish in Berkeley, California and a Benedictine oblate with Saint Gregory's Abbey in Three Rivers, Michigan. He taught at two seminaries and two spiritual direction training programs. He began formal training in Core Shamanism in 2016 through Michael Harner's Foundation for Shamanic Studies, concentrating on shamanic healing modalities. He also studied compassionate depossession work with Elizabeth Bergstrom. Daniel maintains the website http://www.llministries.com for his private practice, Lamb & Lion Spiritual Guidance Ministries. He is the author of *Where Two or Three are Gathered: Spiritual Direction for Small Groups;* and *Light on the Path: Guiding Symbols for Insight and Discernment.*

JOHN R. MABRY

Rev. John Mabry is a United Church of Christ pastor with more than twenty-five years of active ministry. He holds a master's degree in Culture and Creation Spirituality and a doctorate in Philosophy and Religion with concentrations in Hinduism and Taoism. Since 2003 he has experimented with Core Shamanism and regularly incorporates shamanic techniques into his spiritual practice. John is the director of the Chaplaincy Institute's interfaith spiritual direction certificate program in Berkeley, California. He maintains a Facebook account and two websites for his writing—https://www.johnrmabry.com/ for his nonfiction and https://www.jrmabry.com/ for his fiction. He is the author of more than thirty titles, both fiction and nonfiction, including: *Spiritual Guidance Across Religions: A Sourcebook for Spiritual Directors and other People Providing Counsel to People of Differing Faith Traditions;* and *Growing Into God: A Beginner's Guide to Christian Mysticism.*

KATRINA LEATHERS

Rev. Katrina Leathers is an interfaith minister ordained through the Chaplaincy Institute in Berkeley, California. She also completed the Chaplaincy Institute's interfaith spiritual direction program and offers spiritual guidance through her One Circle Ministry. Katrina has a master of arts degree in expressive arts therapy. She teaches an introductory course on shamanic practices with the Chaplaincy Institute. She is a graduate of the Three Year Program of Advanced Initiations in Shamanism and Shamanic Healing through the Foundation of Shamanic Studies. Katrina maintains her ministry website http://onecircleministry.com/ and a Facebook presence at *https://www.facebook.com/OneCircleMinistry/*.

Printed in the USA
CPSIA information can be obtained
at www.ICGtesting.com
LVHW041701231023
761916LV00035B/666